BE THE 5

Digital confidence: a simple process for digital success

RICHARD GODFREY

www.get-known.co.uk

GLOBAL SPEND ON DIGITAL
TRANSFORMATION IS CURRENTLY OVER
£1 TRILLION PER YEAR.
(£1,000,000,000,000)

RESEARCH SHOWS THAT UP TO 95% OF
DIGITAL PROJECTS FAIL TO ADD ANY
BUSINESS VALUE.

BE IN **THE FIVE** PERCENT THAT DO!
YOU CAN'T AFFORD NOT TO!

Praise

"Richard manages to combine the big ideas, smart thinking and technical complexities of digital transformation into an easy to understand vision of how things can and should be. He is both strategic in his understanding of the bigger picture and tactical in how to help you implement changes that work for you."

**— STEEVAN GLOVER
FOUNDER, BREWD MARKETING**

"Richard is a real insider. Inside the issues and challenges of digital transformation; this comes with a deep understanding from working inside local authorities about how to effect meaningful change. He also has previous inside knowledge of the private sector as it fashions new products for the market."

**— ANDREW GRANT
EX-CEO, AYLESBURY VALE DISTRICT COUNCIL**

"For the past 15 years, I have been working in the Knowledge Automation arena. Richard is a breath of fresh air in the industry, not only was he implementing our solution, but he was utilising complementary technology to complement his vision. Richard is one of the good guys and a true digital leader. If you are looking for a safe pair of hands and no-nonsense digital transformation expert, my money would be on Richard."

— **PABLO CASTILLO**
PARTNER ACCOUNT DIRECTOR, VERINT

"We used to jokingly refer to Richard as Digital Jesus. He was clearly doing something very different and had a powerful message to tell all. His knowledge of digital and how it can help businesses is second to none. If you need someone to lead you through the digital minefield then there is no-one better in my opinion than Richard."

— **JON HALLEY**
SENIOR DIRECTOR EMEA, BOUNCEX

"Richard isn't afraid to do things differently. When local government were only looking at legacy suppliers, Richard stepped away and challenged the market to deliver better options, utilising the best in breed cloud solutions to deliver the best outcomes!"

— **CHRISTIAN HOSE**
SALES MANAGER, SPRINKLR

"Richard and I worked together on many projects when AWS was a small player in the UK public sector. His ambition and foresight into how technology could deliver better outcomes for citizens is unparalleled. His work on the projects led to him winning the AWS City on a Cloud award."

— CHRIS HAYMAN
COUNTRY GM, UK PUBLIC SECTOR, AWS

"Richard's name was always at the top of the list when looking for speakers, his no-nonsense approach to his work is refreshing and always stimulates conversations. His knowledge of all things digital marks him out as a true leader within the industry."

— ROB SIMMS
CEO, CAMSS WORLD

Contents

PART 3: BECOMING A CONFIDANT, IMPACTFUL DIGITAL LEADER /219

This book is for:
You

Yes, you. You're curious. You've been intrigued by the title. You want to know more. You're a leader. You want to learn. You want to be efficient. More specifically, this book is for you if:

○ You know digital could give your business the efficiencies and profits you need, even change the whole working culture for the better, but you have no idea how to start making that happen.

○ You need to step up and lead the company through a digital project (but feel hugely out of your depth).

○ You want to be seen as a forward-thinking, innovative leader in your company/industry.

○ You are not from a technical/IT background.

○ You do not want to be left behind.

○ You need your digital projects to deliver real business value.

○ You are unsure of the role digital can play in your business.

- You are currently leading digital projects, but you lack confidence in making decisions and do not understand the outcomes.

- You want to make a difference.

Throughout the coming decade all business and business leaders that want to be successful will need an understanding of technology and digital processes. Businesses that embrace digital tools will grow at a faster rate than those that ignore them and will be in a better position to adopt new business models more quickly.

Embrace digital now and you will set yourself apart from the rest. You will have the knowledge to lead the delivery of impactful digital projects that add real value to your business.

This book will: give you digital confidence

A llow me to let you in on a secret that the industry does not want you to know. Digital is not complicated.

It is actually very easy once you have had it explained to you in simple terms. OK, so the actual core workings of digital are complicated. There are a lot of facets to it. But you do not need to know these. We are not asking you to learn to code. We are not asking you to learn all the acronyms and terminology. What we are going to be looking at is how your business can use digital to become more efficient at what it does.

This book will take you on a journey through digital. We will look at many of the issues that are present today in understanding and delivering digital projects. What it is. Why it is important. Your role. Why it goes wrong so often. We will look at the negative side of digital. The 95% failure rates. The lack of understanding. The lack of agreed outcomes. The problems of implementing new tools. The skillset of your current workforce.

We will look at the positives. What digital can bring to your company when it is done correctly. We will consider the role it plays in shaping your business and workforce for the future. We will look at how it can shape you. Make you a better leader. More knowledgeable. More aware.

In Part 1 of the book we will look at the benefits of digital and what it can bring to your business, and we will also be looking at those failure rates and why so many projects fail to add any business value. In Part 2 I will take you through my Be The Five methodology. We will do it in an easy to understand way, with exercises for you to complete that will improve your knowledge in a logical and easy to understand manner. In Part 3 we will look at what the future holds for your business.

This book will give you the confidence to step up to digital challenges, lead your company through innovation (or pioneer innovation within your company) and create a culture to establish a more motivated, engaged and fulfilled workforce. It will enable you to understand how digital can benefit your business. It will show you how to successfully deliver initiatives. It will give you a model to follow to ensure that you can repeat that success time and time again.

I have cut the jargon out and provided everyday examples that you will find accessible. It is not an IT book for the IT person. This book is for the non-IT business leader that needs to understand the digital world better. We have been obsessed with bringing IT into our businesses and trying to get them to understand how we operate, but we have forgotten that the business also needs to understand IT. In this book I have flipped the norm on its head. It is a book about technology for people who do not understand technology. It is a book for business leaders who know they can do better but do not know how to get there. The book will guide you through the process. We will get there together.

BUT IT IS MORE THAN JUST A BOOK ABOUT DIGITAL.

I founded Syncity in 2019 to develop business leaders to help them to achieve success in delivering digital pro-grammes.

Syn- *derived from Greek means 'together'. The word 'city' comes from the Latin root* 'civitas'*, originally meaning citizenship or community member.*

I want to create a community or 'city' of leaders that work together. Those who want to re-imagine the world we live in through innovative technology. People who are not afraid to challenge the norm. People who inspire others.

Having worked in the public sector for over a decade, I have a passion for delivering better services as efficiently as possible. Bringing communities together to make a dif-ference.

Creating a digital culture is about more than just tech-nology. It can bring new ways of working, with a wider reach and a more balanced lifestyle. It makes the world smaller and more accessible. It gives you opportunities that were never possible just a few years ago. Digital is a social movement.

Companies will evolve, the ones that do well now will be the ones people want to work for in the future. Digital improves staff engagement. It improves well-being and fulfilment. It moves away from presenteeism towards more dynamic ways of working. It improves services for customers and employees.

This is about so much more than profits. It can lead to ecological, social, and environmental change. There is no better time to embrace being digital and to take the opportunity to rewrite the script.

It is time for you to become a confident, impactful digital leader!

think **D**ifferent

be **E**fficient

work **T**ogether

be a **S**ynner!

Introduction

THE PROBLEM

There is very little that you can do in today's world that does not have an element of digital in it somewhere. The ways we shop, manufacture, watch TV, hail taxis, organise holidays, read books, exercise and do pretty much anything else you can think of, right through to some of the most manual jobs, all have digital somewhere in the chain. A lot of the time you will not even notice it, especially if it is done correctly.

The importance of digital and its usage across businesses is only going to increase over time. The ever-changing technology landscape means that there are more and more tools coming to market each year and more options than ever. Keeping up with this changing landscape is hard. What has not changed, though, is the head in the sand approach that a lot of companies have adopted to this. It is estimated that spend on digital transformation in 2023 will be between £2-3 trillion per annum. That figure will only grow as new technologies come to the marketplace.

As large as this number sounds, what is more shocking is that – for digital transformation – research suggests that only 5% of projects meet or exceed expectations. That means that 95% do not.

Imagine if that directly correlates to spend. That means that for every £1,000,000 spent on digital transformation, £950,000 of that is failing to deliver the required outcomes. Now multiply that back up to trillions of pounds and you can see how large a disparity we have in the industry.

If we know that 95p in every £1 spent on digital is used ineffectively, then how do we move forwards? Why are we seeing such huge amounts of waste? What can you do about it?

As a business leader in these times, you now need to be able to have real business conversations with the IT department. You must be able to speak the same language as them. You must be able to challenge them and realise the potential that you now have if you and the business can work efficiently with IT to deliver real business value. You must have a digital strategy that delivers business outcomes and you must understand how and why.

WE ARE NOW AT A CROSSROADS

COVID changed everything. Suddenly digital was at the forefront of business culture. Companies had to change, adapt, embrace digital and change working cultures very rapidly. They had to do this to survive. The ones that did this well had first-mover advantage. Attitudes and pre-conceptions changed overnight. All those things that were not previously possible, suddenly became so. We became a nation of homeworkers. Small businesses rapidly opened online stores and offered delivery services. We used Zoom as a verb to stay in touch with colleagues and loved ones. Suddenly, being in an office was less important. Office hours became more relaxed. Zoom fatigue even became a thing.

Away from digital we saw huge ecological changes as traffic levels plummeted and therefore the associated pollutant levels also did. The waters in Venice cleared. The Himalayas were visible from India for the first time in 30 years. We saw animals reclaiming parts of our cities. It opened our eyes to a different world.

It wasn't enough, though. Digital suddenly became about using Zoom or Teams. We congratulated ourselves on the adoption of these. We lauded IT departments for how quickly they had rolled out solutions. Yet behind this we saw very different results too. Companies that had to furlough staff because they didn't have the right solutions in place. Local government organisations that could only operate at 60% of capacity. Shops that had no online presence going out of business. Solutions that should have been in place years ago showed up our lack of knowledge of technology. Digital goes so much deeper than just how teams communicate. It opens a whole new world of opportunities.

Now is not the time to take your foot off the gas. Digital

evolves and it continues to evolve. You can disrupt the way that you work, and you can disrupt your industry. Or you can be disrupted.

Consider Uber and Netflix. Both these companies have disrupted their industries. There have been casualties in this with some big-name businesses not surviving. Blockbuster were too attached to their late fee model to change in time to compete with Netflix. Uber have disrupted the taxi industry. Kodak have all but been removed from their industry. They saw film and print as their core market as digital cameras were taking over. Airbnb have disrupted the travel industry. Even companies such as Compare the Market have disrupted the industry by giving consumers an easy way of comparing services and costs.

Although digital has played a role in a lot of this disruption, the business model is what has caused the most problems. Sticking rigidly to a model and not being able to adapt to a new model quickly enough has hurt these businesses. Blockbuster were offering online movies before Netflix. They were even offered the Netflix company to purchase. It was not just about the technology. It was their business model. They made a lot of money off late fees. Netflix simply removed these. Netflix were not bought and, in the end, it was their business model and the efficiency they gave customers that saw them grow to the size they are today. Blockbuster could have killed off Netflix many years ago but missed the opportunity.

Although digital is a vital tool in making your business

"

Even if your
industry has
not been
disrupted yet,
it will be.

more efficient, it will only truly benefit you if you can ensure your business model is also correct. In this book we will look at your market and the wider industries to look at where services are going. Keeping an eye on this is crucial to your business and why you need to have that digital knowledge. Even if your industry has not been disrupted yet, it will be.

Digital technology will allow someone at some point to change the business model of your industry. If you do not understand digital and how it will help your business, then you are more likely to be disrupted than to be the disruptor. Use your knowledge to consider how you could be delivering services differently. Consider the types of digital tools that would allow you to make rapid changes to the way you deliver services. Most people have heard of Amazon Retail, but less about Amazon Web Services (AWS). AWS can release up to 100 new tools a year. It is quite hard for the staff to sometimes keep on top of what they offer let alone you. They are not alone in offering more and more new services each year.

Digital improvements cannot be a one-off exercise. It is something you must be doing continuously. You will not keep up with the new releases. Not many people do. You do need to be aware of the company's core offerings, though, and how they could help you. If you are not, then perhaps your competitors are.

Look at Amazon Rekognition. Did you even know this service existed? Would this help you at all? It is one of hundreds of services they provide. What about Amazon

Connect? There is a world of opportunity out there for you, you just need to grab it.

I will mention a lot of the market leaders in this book, but there are hundreds of companies all offering services that might be of help to you. Keep Discovering. Keep seeing what the market is doing. Keep thinking big. Everything is possible. Keep ahead of the pack and disrupt before you are disrupted.

BE A DIGITAL LEADER OF THE FUTURE

Whilst we look at keeping your business ahead of the pack, there is also an opportunity for you. Being a leader who understands digital puts you ahead of your compatriots. It will give you a better understanding of how you can reshape your business for the better.

By thinking differently, you can make changes to your business that bring impactful change. You can have a happier, more engaged, less stressed workforce. You can move to a flexible time and location-based workforce. You can free yourself from mundane tasks. You can spend more time working on the business and not in it. You can focus on the bigger picture. You can focus on the environment, the economy, the welfare of citizens. You can make a real difference to the world.

Let me show you how...

1

My Story

HOW I GOT INTO DIGITAL

Sitting in a very posh boardroom at the British Academy in London in 2016, I had the worst case of Imposter Syndrome that I have ever experienced in my career. I had been invited to a meeting with the Government Office for Science by the No 10 Policy Unit to discuss the Ethics of Artificial Intelligence. I was surrounded by multiple professors, CEO's of tech companies, science advisors, private secretaries. I was in a meeting chaired by Sir Mark Walport, the Government Chief Scientific Adviser at the time. I felt like I was in the wrong room and was unusually quiet for the first time in my life. How had I got myself into this position?

I am not your typical IT or digital worker. In fact, I used to hate computers and could barely turn one on throughout school. Like most people my age, I was introduced to computers at primary school with the BBC Micro and the Domesday Project. The main thing I really remember was the size of the disc that you inserted into the drive, but I can't recall much else (it was huge!). At senior school we used to have computer lessons that, to be honest, bored the life out of me. Luckily, my name was exactly halfway through the two groups our class had been split into. I therefore managed to avoid turning up in the first half of term claiming I thought I was in the second group. When the second group started, I claimed I had been in the first. I am sure the teacher at the time cared little whether I turned up or not anyway. But I was obsessed with sport and that is what filled my life. After all, computers were for those who couldn't play sports, weren't they?

Games consoles were different; I had owned the original Atari that was made of wood. For those of you reading this who are a lot younger than me, yes, that is right: it was made of wood! I then went through the Sega Master System and Mega Drive, spending my sixth-form years playing Tiger Woods Golf, before the advent of the Sony PlayStation, which helped me through the university years playing *SSX Tricky*, a snowboarding game.

At university I really came across computers for the first time, but I still had little interest in them. I was doing a degree in Sport and Exercise Science, so they had limited use for me. They were a functional tool for writing essays. In most cases, we purchased electronic typewriters rather than computers. I remember being introduced to a system called 'email' by my housemate at the time. I just could not understand the theory. If I wanted to message someone, why would I not just call them? Why would I wait two or three days for them to reply? It made no sense to me. I therefore concluded that it would never catch on and so I had little need for an email address.

Moving into my first job after university I started to come across more types of software that I had never had to use before. The first was a Customer Relationship Management (CRM) tool, called Goldmine. I viewed this very much as a Rolodex, calendar and task list rolled into one and it was how I managed all my work. After a week's training on the system, I decided it was going to be far too complicated to use. However, within a few weeks, it became second nature and I was suggesting improve-ments to our IT team (if a team can be two people!). The second system was called Lotus Notes, and back to that all-important email!

I had my first business email address, although I had very little use for it, except for chatting to other people within the company and avoiding doing any real work. I also now had a personal email address. If memory serves, it was something like rjgodfrey69@hotmail.com. I used 69 as that was my house address and, because I was 20 years old, I thought it was funny – sadly not true. I think that was also the year we all got very excited about

Friends Reunited and started to contact friends from school that we had drifted apart from, mostly to be nosey.

For the next ten years, I had very little interaction with computers on a meaningful scale. I worked in the public sector and used some very specific software for my role, before moving to the private sector and using more software specific to the role. Looking back now, it is easy to see how similar all these systems were. At the time they were just a tool to do my job, nothing more. I had no interest in how they worked or hung together. Turning it on and off was pretty much the limit of my knowledge.

My life changed when I moved to Peterborough City Council and completed an internal move to manage the newly outsourced ICT contract. I had to learn technology and I had to learn it quickly. It was necessary to be able to challenge, understand and approve any work that was being completed as I was the link between IT and the business. I needed a wide range of knowledge to cover all aspects of the service. It helped that I had an excellent teacher, Ross Mardell, who was able to break down the aspects of IT into easy to understand terms. I remember my first lesson being a drawing of the trenches of the First World War. My second being about how phones sent your voice to another phone and it still sounded like you and not a robot! I really was starting from basics.

However, I also partly credit my 'digital' career to timing. IT was at a bit of a turning point during that time. The first iPhone had been recently released, there was talk of this strange 'cloud' and the idea that IT could help

deliver transformation was gaining traction. Digital transformation was becoming a buzz phrase. Had I been in
the role a few years previously, then I may well have lost
interest and moved away from the industry. However,
here I was, fresh faced to IT. The market was starting to
look interesting and it was becoming clear to me that
technology and digital would be the driving force in business over the years to come. Someone had to grasp the
opportunity that it gave us, and that someone was going
to be me.

Around 2013, I began speaking to a company called
Cityfibre, who were looking to invest in cities to improve
their fibre infrastructure (internet). They had bought out a
previous company that had failed to deliver on its prom-
ises on the few contracts it had. Although sceptical at first,
I was soon convinced that there was a real opportunity
here for the city. I had already started planning for how the
council could deliver its services using digital tools, but I
knew this was not enough. For real change to happen, we
had to look at the city as a whole. In November 2013, the
council signed a deal with Cityfibre to invest up to £30m
into the digital infrastructure of the city. This was on top of
a BT contract to improve connectivity, and an agreement
with Gigaclear to reach some of the remotest areas followed. Peterborough was genuinely going to be one of
the best-connected cities in the world. This would give
the city the opportunity to grow a digital sector, help local
businesses to use the internet better and maybe draw
companies away from London and Cambridge. It now

gives residents access to some of the fastest internet speeds in the world. It also saved the council hundreds of thousands of pounds on network costs.

At this time, the council was also being hit by the government's austerity plans and were looking at large scale service delivery changes to save millions of pounds a year. It was also clear that if we wanted to market Peterborough as a digital city then the council should also lead the way and offer world class digital services.

THE STRATEGY THAT CHANGED EVERYTHING

It was around this time that a meeting with a consultant, James Herbert, really opened my eyes and changed everything for me. It was not a meeting I was even in. My boss at the time was meeting with a company to discuss various aspects of the council. I joined for the last few minutes and mentioned what I was thinking of doing. The response was, 'Have you looked at Salesforce?' I had not. To be honest, I had never even heard of them. The next two weeks were pretty much spent reading their website, looking at their systems, watching their customer stories and looking at their ecosystem. It was clear that here was part of the answer to the council's financial problems.

Between James and I, we wrote one of the first Cloud Technology strategies to be seen in local government. The strategy would see the council move away from legacy providers in the sector. They would work with new, more modern cloud software companies that were designed to work together. This would join up the services across the council and deliver a richer data experience that would help future service planning. For the first time, a public sector agent was going to embrace what were seen as private sector tools in helping them deliver more efficient services. More importantly, though, the new software was flexible enough that the users (staff in this case) would be able to build processes that worked for them. They would not have to stick to rigid legacy technology processes that were outdated and contained a lot of wasted effort. We had over £12m to save and so we had to make our processes as efficient as possible. These days you will hear lots of talk of Service Design or User Centred Service Design, as if this is a new thing. It is, however, now becoming more popular although, amazingly, it is not how software was previously built. Design it with your end users, whether internal or external, and you will achieve better results.

Once the strategy was formally launched, I was in great demand to give talks at conferences. This was not natural to me, and I was terrified at the first one. I wore a black jumper over my shirt just in case I sweated too much and had to ask for a bottle of cold water to hold as my palms were sweating and I feared dropping the microphone. However, once the microphone was in my hand, there was no stopping me. I quickly realised that attendees were there to listen and learn and not to try and call me out. I was still terrified of people thinking I was a fraud in the technology world because of my non-technical background. This passed when it became clear that no-one else really knew more than me about this 'cloud' thing and I could caveat every talk with it being right for Peterborough, meaning no-one could disagree. I spoke in Germany and America as well as multiple times in the UK. I became a judge for awards. I was one of the first Digital Leaders 100 members and I got invited to the Houses of Parliament. I then found myself being invited to the previously mentioned meeting with the Government Office for Science by the Number 10 Policy Unit.

THE MOST INTIMIDATING MEETING

I mention this meeting as a key point. Not because of the meeting itself but because of the conversations that were held during it. The problem with a room full of professors and scientists is that they are professors and scientists. I would liken them to a lot of technology experts. This is not to say anything bad. They are generally very logical and very technical people, but they are not always able to relate that to the real world and real-world scenarios. They used technical terms that only they understood. They were proud of how clever they were and how big the words they used were. Bundle this together with acronyms that I have long forgotten the component words for, and suddenly I found myself in quite an intimidating position. I held my own and gave real-world examples of how artificial intelligence could really impact lives, both positively and negatively, and changed some of the context of the meeting. After the meeting, I spoke to the No 10 Policy Unit about feeling out of place and they explained that I was there on purpose to ground some of the conversations in reality. I could also translate the technical into simple examples. There are many people that I have worked with that would have frozen in the same meeting. It is similar to how when we discuss digital with people who believe it is not their job they also freeze. In today's world, though, it is everybody's job.

A large part of the reason as to why I can translate effectively is because I am not great at English. I do not use big words. Mainly because I can't as I do not know what they mean. But I can take the technical terms and break them down into real-world language that has meaning to people outside of the sectors. I try not to overcomplicate anything. Technology is full of its own terminology and acronyms. It can look complicated and confusing. It does not need to be. I make the process as simple to understand as possible.

Excluding non-experts from a conversation through the language that is used is one of the major reasons that digital projects fail to deliver business benefits. It is one that often goes unchallenged and ignored. As well as having to learn digital from a technical perspective, I also had to learn to be the intermediary between digital and the business, bringing the two together in a meaningful way.

I left my role at Peterborough a couple of years later.

By which point I had completed the UK conference circuit. I had attended and spoken at conferences in the USA and Europe. I had my own Customer Success videos with software providers (never film these after ten days in Las Vegas). I had featured in *Forbes* magazine with the work we were doing in Peterborough and had been named by *Computer Weekly* as one of their Rising Stars.

In fact, I was the digital and data lead in an incredible team that won the World's Smartest City award. In the process, we beat Dubai, Buenos Aires and other much larger, more internationally recognised cities. In addition, I won the AWS City on a Cloud competition alongside Los Angeles and Washington DC. At that time, we were using Amazon Web Services to analyse data from weather stations that were being installed in local schools. We wanted to interest the children in the environment whilst at the same time doing 'maths by stealth' through data analysis. An extra benefit was that the council could also use the data to predict service demand based on weather patterns. After achieving all of this, and making a difference locally, I really felt like I had finally proven myself in the industry.

DIGITAL EFFICIENCY IN THE PUBLIC SECTOR

One of the key elements that we look at throughout the book is the focus on using digital systems to be more efficient as a business. My background is largely in the public

"

You need
to be looking
at a wide
range of
industries.

sector and you may think that that has little relevance to your business, but you would be wrong. The models and tools that I've worked with and implemented are hugely popular in the private sector and, when you boil issues down to their nuts and bolts, you find that most industries have similar issues and can learn lots from each other.

I used to work quite closely with a company called Okta that focused on access management and security for cloud-based tools. I spoke at several of their conferences and events and often shared the stage with the then CIO of Gatwick Airport. You would think that we'd both had very different experiences, but we had similar stories, especially around legacy suppliers, a limited marketplace of suppliers, needing to use data better, and becoming more efficient as a business. The more we spoke, the clearer our parallels became. Ultimately, his role was to help make the airport more efficient and help improve their income, mine was to make the council more efficient and deliver services with a smaller budget. However, the solutions and the tools that we were both looking at were very comparable.

I had a similar experience at an HR conference in London, where it was only private sector attendees, but the overall models that I described were applicable to any business looking at harnessing and using their data better to deliver better experiences, either internally or externally. I had a long conversation at the end of my talk with an employee from a large well-known supermarket about how they could look at a similar approach.

Therefore, I talk about looking at different sectors in the methodology that follows. You cannot just be looking at the same industry that you are in and thinking that you will learn enough from it. You need to be looking at a wide range of industries, including central and local government, to see what works and what solutions are being delivered. Do not be narrow in your research. The public sector is an excellent starting point, given the cuts that all councils have seen hit their budgets over the last decade. Of course, there are exceptions, there are in any industry, but there is a lot of good work and examples that you could look at in delivering your own experiences, including new delivery models. If you want to become an efficient well-oiled machine, then research the right examples that can help you to deliver that.

BRIDGING THE DIVIDE

Syncity was born out of a desire to cut through the noise of the digital industry. It's a very divisive noise, between those who understand and those who don't. It often seems like it's designed to keep the divide in place. Keep buying our tools and we'll keep pushing for digital transformation through our marketing. All digital developments are born from the providers. They are leading the way and it's time to reverse this. It's about the customers and their needs. Solutions such as 5G were pushed and promoted by the vendors but not requested by the buyer. Smart Cities are promoted by platform providers. It's time for this to stop and the power to return to those who are using digital to change their business or environment for the better. We need to stop listening to the hype and focus on the outcomes.

There is a constant stream of digital information pushed to social media. It's written by marketing teams selling products. So much of it is untrue or unproven. Yet it keeps getting shared. There is so much bullshit in the industry that it's hard to cut through this noise and see it for what it really is. As I've said, digital isn't complicated, but it does take some effort to learn about it and to challenge the preconceptions. This is where my passion comes to the fore. I am constantly challenging. Constantly putting my head above the parapet to speak up. I see digital strategy after digital strategy that I would consider to be appallingly ineffective. Backed by companies that really don't know what they're doing but are happy to take your money. It's all possible because of the divide they keep in place between IT and the business.

The divide will only truly be bridged when the business starts to take more of an interest in digital and the possibilities it can bring. No longer can you bury your head in the sand.

My passion is to create a city of Synners – a community that aims to be a thorn in the side to the industry, holding them accountable for their claims and using digital for the greater good. We can create better services, better systems and a better world through a better approach to digital. Embrace it. Look at the bigger picture. Bridge those divides.

I want a community of people that think differently, that want to be efficient, that will work together. It is only by creating this that we can really make a difference. Start small, by all means. Change your business. Communicate better with colleagues. Grow their interest and together we can make a huge difference to our cities, communities and environments.

I love the outdoor life – I love nature and I love being on the sea – so I want Syncity to be making a real difference to the world. I've aligned my business to two of the UN's Sustainable Development Goals because of this. It's ultimately about the bigger picture and the improvements we can make. Digital can have both a positive and a negative effect on the environment if it is not understood properly. Let's bridge the divide. Let's bring the business closer to IT. Let's use digital to help everyone. Improve your company. Improve your city. Improve your environment. Let's create a community of people that work together. Let's create a Syncity.

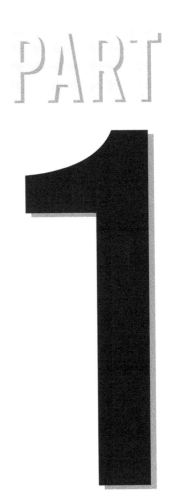

PART

1

Digital – So Much Potential, So Misunderstood

INTRODUCTION TO PART 1

It is all well and good throwing stats out there from the internet but without any context they can be misleading. With only 5% of digital projects adding any business value we need to understand why that is the case. There is a whole industry out there looking at digital failure and the reason behind it. Funnily enough, most people understand the problem and have a solution for it, yet we still see so many issues. If we totally remove failure, then what will they do instead?

Much of the blame has been shifted away from the technology and onto the people and the culture. But this misses a huge number of underlying issues that also contribute to the failure rate. To understand the failures, we first have to understand the benefits that can be delivered from digital. Once we understand why so many businesses are looking to implement it, we can then look at the issues that they come across. From there, building a solution becomes much simpler.

Therefore, in this section we will focus on the benefits that digital can bring to your business before moving onto the failures. We will explore some of the myths around digital and what they really mean. Let us look at where companies are going, why they are going there and what is holding them back from succeeding on this journey. It will make a lot more sense to you when you understand their ambitions.

Why Digital
is the Answer

INTRODUCTION

Understanding digital and what it can do for your business will set you apart from the crowd. The Be The Five methodology gives you a framework to walk through, steps that will give you the knowledge and confidence to embrace digital within your organisation.

Digital allows you to look at and review your current processes to see where you can become more efficient.

By thinking about efficiencies, you will also be able to grow and scale your company more quickly and easily than before.

"

Almost everything is possible. It normally comes down to budget, time, and value.

A leader confident in digital brings more opportunities to their business. Digital enables growth. It enables improved customer service. It enables better insights.

Like your life outside of the business, digital is everywhere. Digital use is growing. Customers expect options around service delivery.

There are so many instances of good and bad practice with digital that you can learn from.

Open your mind to the possibilities that digital can bring your business. Look at best practice from all industries. When I first started in digital, I was not limited by my knowledge of how technology worked. I questioned everything. Now it is your turn. Be bold. Have ambitious plans. Almost everything is possible. It normally comes down to budget, time, and value.

Remember that a Rosetta space probe landed on a moving comet, millions of miles from Earth after over a decade in space. That was ambition.

It is time to look at the possibilities that digital brings.

GETTING DIGITAL RIGHT

There is obviously going to be a lot to take in. Whether you have a good knowledge of the subject already or are new to understanding digital. One thing you cannot hide from is how crucial it is going to be for your business. It is important for you to understand the basics and to be able to see how digital can help your business. If you are going to invest in new digital tools then you need to ensure that you know not only that your investment is going to deliver real business benefits but how and why, so the benefits of this can be measured. You can no longer sit back and leave digital to others. At the very least you must be able to bring IT to the table and to have real conversations with them. The business needs to learn more about IT and IT need to learn more about the business, and it is your role to facilitate this.

Through the methodology in this book you will go through a period of research and learning that will put you in a prime position to approve the strategy that is going to help you to deliver your goals. Learn where you want the company to go, and how digital will help you to get there, and you will be in a good place to make sure that you are getting digital right.

BUSINESS BENEFITS OF DIGITAL

1. Digital makes data more accessible

One of the key elements of today's digital world is data. In fact, let's change that – data is *the* key element of digital. The reason we have computer software is to capture or share data and turn it into information. Even typing this book now, I am putting data into my laptop to be stored and used as information for you to read. Data is the life-blood of everything. The internet transfers data. Software captures data. Our smartphones allow us to mobilise our data. Social media lets us interact with our data. We turn that data into information that we can benefit from.

The fact that a lot of this data is now captured digitally does not make it any different to how it was captured previously. Before there were CRM systems and mobile phones, we had the Rolodex, we had the Filofax, we had diaries, we had phone books, we had address books. All we have done is digitise this data and made it more efficient for you to access. You no longer need to carry these books around. In most cases, these days you just need a smartphone to hold this information. In fact, most digital concepts are just taking everyday activities and digitising both them and the data that is captured. There is nothing really that complicated about most of it from a high level. Even Blockchain, which confuses so many people, is just a ledger at heart. Yes, the technology behind it is relatively complicated, but you do not need to know how it works, just what it is. And, as you will guess, the key to an accurate ledger is the data. A ledger is only as good as the data it holds. In other words, make sure the information in the ledger is correct.

What digital gives you, for now, is the opportunity to do more with your data through having it more accessible. We can see deeper insights into our customers or how our business is delivering. It can be made very visual, using Business Intelligence tools, and easier to understand. A lot more so than just seeing numbers in a spreadsheet. One of the key benefits is that a lot of this data can now be accessed in real time. Think about how you currently receive reports in your business. In some cases, these may have taken weeks to pull together all the correct information and, by the time you read it, you are looking at last month's information. Not what is happening right now in your business.

Imagine they did that with the Premier League football table. They would make you wait a few days for the league table to be updated and then send it to you via email as a spreadsheet. Sounds ludicrous, but that is exactly how many businesses are still operating. What actually happens with the Premier League table is that it's updated every couple of minutes as goals are scored and results change, so you can see an 'as it stands' version of it. No more waiting around to receive the results. It is this level of insight and speed that you want to be able to delve into to improve your company and make it as efficient as possible. With the use of digital tools, you can analyse everything from a few lines of data to millions of rows, relatively cheaply and easily. And, as digital becomes more like a utility in the way it is paid for, you can analyse the data and then switch it off. Only paying for computing power that you have used. Key to becoming efficient as a business is going to be your ability to learn how to be efficient with your data.

2. Data management brings efficiency

With data being key within your business, there is an easy model to follow to ensure that you are giving it the right considerations. It will enable you to look at digital projects and the benefits that data will bring you. If you have looked at the circular economy, then you may have come across the Ellen MacArthur Foundation. Their mission is to accelerate the transition to a circular economy. The Foundation states that there are three key principles to consider when looking at a circular economy and these are:

○   Design out waste and pollution

○   Keep products and materials in use

○   Regenerate natural systems

What is clear is that you can apply the same principles and thinking to data and how it is used across your businesses. The three principles can be applied to your data and how you look at your systems and digital projects.

DESIGN OUT THE WASTE AND POLLUTION OF DATA

Many key systems are standalone and not designed to share data across services. Through implementing a digital platform ecosystem, both services and systems data can be used more widely throughout your business. Siloed data that is used once and then 'wasted' can be designed out of your systems. You can ensure that all departments have access to the same data and share the same relevant information. Where possible, data created by one system or service should be used to improve all the services you deliver and not be 'lost'. If we are also looking to remove pollution from our data, then you will be looking at how you can now cleanse your data. Remove duplicate records and bad data, whether out-dated, misinformed or copied incorrectly.

KEEP DATA IN USE

Keeping data in use is vital to achieving business effi-ciencies. Sales should be ensuring that their valuable customer data is not lost when the customer moves from the Sales cycle into the Service cycle. Do not make your service team start from scratch. I have worked with numerous public sector services where data is used by one team and not another, when it could clearly play a mutually beneficial role.

With machine learning and artificial intelligence, the machines are reliant on an ever-increasing amount of good data being fed into them. This enables them to learn and refine the responses and answers given. All AI solutions can only ever be as good as the data they are utilising. There needs to be a constant feed of good quality data for the machines to learn from.

REGENERATE NATURAL SYSTEMS

In circular economy terms, the focus is on improving the natural environment. For you, you are looking at improv-ing your business environment. Having better access to and better use of your data can help you become more efficient with the resources that you already have, without necessarily needing more. These resources could be people, services, or equipment.

I cannot over-emphasise how important your data is and will be. It is vital to your business and will help drive efficiency and everything that comes with it. If you can understand data, then you are halfway to understanding digital.

3. Digital helps you scale and grow

Businesses that learn to use digital tools efficiently will place themselves ahead of the pack in their industry. Remember, we are talking about how to efficiently run your business, utilising for your benefit everything that the internet brings and enables you to do differently than 20 years ago. Think across everything that you can possibly use. There's social media, YouTube, TikTok, WhatsApp and hundreds of other tools aimed at market engagement. You can shoot a 4k video at home on your phone, edit it and upload it in minutes and have a digital asset available for all your customers for evermore. The opportunities have never been so great. The fact that most people only think of digital as social media and marketing is where they are going wrong. All your systems can now be delivered via the internet. You do not need large IT setups anymore.

The reason that companies such as Airbnb and Uber have managed to grow and scale globally so rapidly is because they have used the internet. They not only market and sell their services on it but they have also built and developed their services on tools that are internet based. Tools that are bought and paid for like utilities, so you are paying for what you use. This enables you to start small and grow rapidly. Companies and services like Amazon Web Services, Google Cloud Platform and Microsoft Azure have access to a global network of infrastructure that can be utilised and turned on and off as you need. For Uber and Airbnb, they would never have been able to afford to buy the infrastructure that they needed to go global in the time they did without spending hundreds of millions of pounds. Uber would not have been able to add Uber Eats so easily without it. Digital tools and the internet allowed them to scale and grow at a rate that they were comfortable with, adding new locations and services as it made sense to.

You may not have a desire to go global, but you should be looking at how these companies have made the most of the tools that the internet has now given them and apply them to your own situation. Look at how paying for digital tools can move you to a more efficient model of paying through a monthly revenue model over a large capital expenditure.

A good example of this is UCAS for university allocations. Over the course of a year, UCAS runs its services at a fairly regular rate and then, once a year, they have a massive spike as students look up what places they have been offered. If UCAS were to buy the amount of infrastructure they would need to cover the spike then they would need to spend thousands of pounds, possibly even hundreds of thousands. This infrastructure would also be left redundant for the other 364 days of the year. With digital it is the opposite. You can pay for the minimum and then only pay extra over and above your normal rate and only for the period you need it. It is not really that different to your electricity usage at home. You have a steady rate coming to the house constantly. If you have a smart meter you will know what this is. Then you want a cup of tea and you need to spike your usage for three minutes whilst the kettle boils. The electricity company let you have the extra electricity and then you pay for it at the end of the month. Those with smart meters will turn all unnecessary electricity off when items are not being used to save money. You can do the same with your infrastructure.

Not all digital tools work in exactly the same way, from a monetary perspective. They have similarities in that, even if you pay annually, adding more users does not require you to buy any more hardware to cope with the capacity. You just buy additional licences. No digital software company will say that you cannot have an extra user because they have run out of capacity. They are designed to scale and, in becoming efficient as a business, you should be able to grow and shrink your infrastructure as needed. If you have static costs, then you are not going to be making the most of your estate.

4. Digital brings you long-term gains

Let's get straight to the point here. Digital is going to cost you money. How much depends on what you want to achieve. Realising the benefits of it might also not be immediate or even immediately obvious. There will be some instances where you can instantly replace a manual process with an automated one and save money. The airline app is a good example as it clearly saves money on printing and mailing costs for the airline. Sometimes it is about time efficiency. A friend of mine recently messaged me to say:

'We turned on Active Campaign this afternoon… holy shit! Amazing piece of software, working with Zapier, Stripe, Xero, Outlook and our Wordpress site. The automation has saved us so many hours, wish we had done it years ago.'

Now this was all about automating a lot of his sales processes. To be clear, I did not do the work and am not claiming to have, but we had spoken a lot about automating his tasks. The return on investment was about his time saving and being able to focus on the more essential business tasks. However, he is also now selling more than he ever was before due to the automated sales process he has set up. It was an unexpected upturn for his business. What it has also allowed is for him to collect much better information on his customers to be able to give a better service further down the line. He wanted a relatively quick short-term gain on his time as he was spending too long on administrative tasks. He has found that he now has a long-term gain in his order book. This was a few short processes that were automated. Nothing really that clever at all. He had a good idea of where he wanted the company to go and knew where he had to spend his time, so he was investing for the future. It just happened much more quickly than he expected.

That is really the point here. You are investing in digital for the long-term benefit of your company. It might be a CRM system, so that you capture better data and information. It may take a few years for all that data to come to fruition, but you will be in a much stronger position when it does. Too often it is short-term projects for short-term gains. Or, more accurately, when you do not see short-term gains you stop what you are doing. Sometimes you will have accidental gains that you were not expecting. Back to the disrupt or be disrupted concept. If your competitors are collecting data now, in three years they will be ahead of you and in a better position to take advantage of market conditions or changes that they need to make. You need to be thinking long term and where you want to be in five years. What do you need to do today to get there? Those businesses that are only thinking about short-term gains will fail.

Short-term gains are of course of benefit but you cannot always measure time efficiencies. These should be aligned to the business and where you want to get to long term. Simple things like automating processes may mean you can hire a salesperson over an admin person.

It may mean you do not need to hire anyone. It may help make your current teams better. Think about your business, where you want to be in five years, and how you can get there in the most efficient way.

CUSTOMER BENEFITS OF DIGITAL

1. Digital gives you consistency

Quite possibly you have started to investigate how joining your systems up could give you a better experience internally. In doing so, you should also have found out how this joins services up for customers. What you will find in a lot of businesses is a lack of consistency with how the customer is treated. We all know, or should know, about sales leads and prospects – having a funnel and taking those potential customers through to a sale – but can you say for sure that at each stage of the process your customers are getting the same experience and the same message?

I have been in plenty of sales meetings where I have been presented with information that conflicts or differs from information that I have seen on the company website. I have also been sold on a message about how much the company cares about its customers and then, as soon as you have purchased, you get lost somewhere in the system and never hear from anyone again.

By thinking of your systems as an ecosystem to manage your data you can start to build that relationship with your customers. Not only can you take them through a consistent sales process, you can also deliver the experience that keeps them coming back for more.

How often have you phoned the customer service centre of a utility company with an issue and, having had to phone back a second time, found yourself repeating the same information over again? Then you are passed to another department and go through the same process. Then you receive a letter a few days later that seems to have ignored everything you have told them. It is very frustrating. It is also a common problem that many of you will have come across time and time again. You are sold a cheaper utility tariff but often the trade-off is a really poor customer experience. By creating the right ecosystem of joined-up systems you can avoid this. You can ensure that you are giving the best experience in a consistent manner and the hand- off from one service to the next is seamless.

Salesforce sell their main CRM product in a variety of setups. The two core ones are Sales and Service. That means within the same environment you can have systems designed for your specific team's efficiency. At the same time, you can ensure that all the sales data you have gathered on a customer can be easily accessed by the service or customer support teams. If internally you cannot share the same data, then how do you expect to serve your customers consistently well?

Having consistent processes, through a consistent ecosystem of tools, will help you to deliver a consistent level of service to your customers. You can use digital to help remove your business silos.

2. Digital data brings you efficiencies

The efficiency of how you use your data is key to your success going forwards, and there are many ways it can be used. Look at Uber. Their app looks at users, available cars, and traffic to have dynamic pricing of journeys. Sometimes you win and sometimes you lose. It is your choice to have a more efficient experience in ordering an Uber than perhaps hailing a cab where the prices are more fixed. That choice sits with you as the customer. Compare that to Facebook, who as most people now know thanks to the US elections, handle vast amounts of your data and your profile interests. In the main, this is to increase advertising revenue on the site. Despite the outrage, people keep using it. It is a free platform after all. The price you pay is that your information is used and sold. They can make more money from advertising than they could by removing marketing and asking subscribers to pay a monthly fee.

Amazon will recommend you items based on your interests, buying habits or habits of buyers with a similar profile to yourself. There are complex algorithms in the background working all this out. They are not doing this for your benefit, even if it feels like it. Even sites such as Trivago, Compare the Market and Kayak are all pulling data from various sources and then presenting it in an easy to understand way. They all collect personal data at the same time they complete the searches. Data, and how you use it, is really going to be key to moving forwards over the next decade. Do not focus on the systems as much as the data they hold and what you do with it. Look at the companies out there, such as Netflix, that saw the internet as a new, more efficient way to deliver content (data) directly to you. They now have your subscription data and information on the types of movies and shows that are popular. They can ensure they are pushing the right type of content onto the platform and are now able to create their own content they know will be popular.

One of the key points to consider here is how the data you collect is going to be able to give you a return whilst also giving the customer a better experience.

You can look at the best example here – reward cards. All the major supermarkets have them. Each time you shop you scan your card and then have points allocated to you. Each month you then receive a booklet with a set of discount vouchers on certain foods. Maybe some cash vouchers too, spend over £50 and get £5 off, and possibly some buy one get one free offers too. As a customer, you probably think that this is excellent customer service. As a business, the supermarket is capturing all sorts of information about you and your shopping habits. This allows them to specifically target you with individual products that are the same as you have bought before, or they are very similar products that people with similar profiles have bought. Often these are new to market products that they are enticing you to buy. They are constantly looking at their data to 'help' you spend more with them and retain you as a loyal customer. They are collecting data on customers but receiving a benefit for it. This enables the supermarket to increase their revenue through using their data wisely whilst also keeping customers loyal.

Similarly, Yo! Sushi have a sensor on each plate of food that they serve. This allows the company to track in real time which plates of food are being purchased across the country. They can then adjust their orders from food suppliers accordingly. This makes their supply chain much more efficient and enables them to rarely run out of popular items. They do not overbuy ingredients and limit food waste. Although this may not look like a customer benefit, as it is about their costs, it does mean that when you go to their restaurant the chance of them not having a dish you like is quite low, giving you a better customer experience.

Transport for London. They introduced the Oyster card in 2003, making it easier for customers to travel around the London transport system. They removed the need to buy paper tickets whilst offering reduced prices for the take-up of the card. This already gives them a saving from reduced printing. However, not only did they make it more time and cost efficient for their customers, it also gave them access to a host of new data on how customers were using the network. The data available helps them to best meet demand and give a better service. These may be small incremental changes but understanding where people are travelling to and from and when, in real time, is useful information for a transport company.

Even car park companies have been more efficient with data. Companies such as Ringo, and the many other car park apps, allow customers to pay by card and not have to find cash. They don't have to walk and queue at a pay booth when it's wet and are sent a reminder when their session is expiring. It allows them to top up without running back to their car to add another ticket to their windscreen. It also allows the car park operator to have less cash to collect from machines and then process. It is easier to monitor the car parks and to understand how people are using them, how often and for how long. Again, all useful information for a car park operator.

Every example provides a benefit to the customer. It also provides a benefit to the company providing the service. That is what you should now be aiming for.

3. Digital personalises services

Data collection and usage is now allowing for services to become more personalised. If we go back to the loyalty card example, the supermarket that sends out their discount vouchers at the end of the month can now send an individually printed set of vouchers to each person. (I will not go into the fact they do not need to print them!) The vouchers you receive may be different to the ones that your neighbour receives. This increases the likelihood of you returning to the shop to buy from them. Think about it logically. If you have shopped for years in the same supermarket and always bought Lurpak, then 50p off Flora probably is not going to entice you. Personal data allows shops to be much more targeted than before.

If you look at the 2016 US election, what Donald Trump did exceptionally well was use Facebook data to message his supporters and potential voters. He was sending a personalised message to each person rather than doing blanket adverts. He was able to do this quickly and easily. Even if the overarching message remained the same, the actual advert could be made much more personal based on the information that they held about you, so each person received a slightly different version of it. He played the social media and data game incredibly well. This ultimately built a big enough following to secure him the presidency, despite any of the negative stories and issues that were raised against him.

In the UK, during the COVID-19 pandemic lockdown, most households received a letter from the Prime Minister. Every single household received the exact same letter at a cost of millions of pounds that could have been used elsewhere. No personalisation. No allowance for age, location, or health. The government just did not have that type of information to hand. The likelihood is that 80% of the letters went in the bin within seconds of coming through the front door. Had the letter been personal to you, and had information about your current situation, then you would have been more likely to read it and pay attention.

Business is the same. Even email headers that start

Dear Sir or Dear Madam are a problem; if you know who I am then address it to me. I am more likely to read an email to Dear Richard than I am to Dear Sir. Even worse is, Dear <insert name here>. It reflects badly on your company if you have someone's information and you do not offer them a personal experience. A letter that comes through my letterbox addressed to 'Homeowner' does not even get opened as I know it is a blanket marketing document. You should now be able to start to look towards offering your customers a much more personalised service. As such, the opportunity to retain them as a customer has never been greater.

4. Digital helps customers help themselves

In many cases, to promote digital efficiency, you will often find that giving the customer the tools to complete the job themselves is the best option. Doing this in a way that makes them then thank you for the experience will lead to success. Think about how Airlines let you print your own tickets or download your boarding card to your phone, or how supermarkets provide self-service check-outs. You will be amazed how grateful customers are to be able to carry out tasks by themselves that you used to do for them. I am always amazed how the messaging of this is all about the customer and never a mention of the internal efficiencies and savings, and yet it is this DIY approach that is accepted without question.

You need to consider how you can help people help themselves, whether that be customers or staff, and how efficient that can make you. Internally, they may help themselves by gaining more knowledge of digital, understanding their data better and automating aspects of their work. Externally, simply by having customers carrying out tasks that you previously had to do for them. As long as the experience is not only more efficient but also better for the user, then they'll be able to complete these tasks with ease and be happy to do so.

The focus for you then will be on digital efficiency. It is time to stop talking about digital transformation and having conversations led by the industry and focus on your own needs as a business. Use digital technology to give you and your customers the most efficient experience that you can. If that ultimately leads to transforming your industry then that is great, but if not then concentrate on yourself and what you offer.

BENEFITS TO STAFF

1. Digitising your processes

Processes are all about a transfer of data or information. We want that transfer to be as smooth as possible. These processes can be both internal and external or a mix of both. Whilst looking for digital efficiencies, you will learn a lot about the processes that you have across your organisation. You might find that some of these processes could be replaced, improved, or automated by using digital tools and configuring them to work for you. It often amazes me how little attention is paid to these processes and how often I hear that something is done a particular way as the person sat next to them told them to do it that way. They were taught by the person that was there before them and so on. At no point are a lot of these processes challenged or improved.

Digital now gives you the opportunity to do this. You can look at other theories and methodologies, such as the Theory of Constraints and Lean or even Six Sigma, then apply this knowledge against what digital tools can bring you. This will put you in a good place. As always, use them as a framework not a hard and fast rule.

Sadly, I enjoy watching *Inside the Factory* on BBC television. I don't watch it to see how amazed Gregg Wallace is when a can of beans is filled from the bottom up, but to see the time and effort that has obviously gone into the process of manufacturing a product. Some of the machines are ingenious. Everyday items that we take very much for granted go through an incredible process, often at incredible speed, to make it to the shops for us to buy. It is also incredible, in most cases, how little human interaction there is in these processes. There is always some, but often it is around quality control or at the start or end of the process only. Yet I go into businesses and offices all the time where very little thought has been given to the processes that are in place. These are often old and outdated and follow old ways of working. Watch the beans or soup episodes. Imagine the can is your data. Look how efficiently it moves through the process. Are your processes as smooth as this?

I once completed an audit at Peterborough and found a typewriter still in use in one department. It did not last much longer. I also remember telling HR I was replacing their system and was thanked as it was so poor. Not once had they come and asked me for a new system, though. They were just struggling on as that was how it had always been. Well, not anymore. You will learn the knowledge and skills to put proper plans in place to become an efficient machine and use digital to improve those processes. Watch *Inside the Factory*, or any large-scale engineering programme, and see how much time and effort is spent on the processes and then ask yourself if you have given them the necessary time and thought. Let the efficiency effect take place and thrive with your newfound knowledge and skills.

There are lots of companies that specialise in improving processes. Find ones that understand your industry and work with them. Remember, though, digital does not solve everything. I have advised a local authority that the best solution to their process was a pen and paper. Digital will help with most things, but not everything has to be done that way.

Review your processes, review what you know about digital and then bring the two together.

2. Automate the distractions

As you look to invest in new technologies, such as chatbots, RPA, AI and business intelligence, then the cost of the IT service will naturally increase. However, you are introducing these tools to make savings. To make efficiencies. To improve customer service. To grow or scale your business. As I have mentioned, IT is a service department to your company. They are giving you the tools to make the company better at what it does.

Does that mean that you do not need as many people if the machines are taking over? Are machines and robots going to take everyone's jobs?

The answer is probably yes. They have been for centuries. At least some of your jobs, or elements of your job. But this is a good thing. They will remove the mundane and repetitive tasks leaving you to focus on the real business value tasks. They can remove the tasks that distract you from the real work. Let us go back in time to before the Industrial Revolution and the combine harvester. If you wanted your field of hay cutting, you would have employed an army of people armed with scythes to go into the field and manually cut the hay. Then one day in 1826 the Reverend Patrick Bell invented a machine to reap the hay. People were replaced with a machine pulled by horses. The first minimum viable product (MVP) version of a combine harvester. Improvements over time have led to combine harvesters today being incredible pieces of machinery. There is not an army of people standing next to the fields today, scythes in hand, complaining that machines have taken their jobs. People adapted. Some would have tended the horses. Some would learn how to fix the machines. Some would learn how to run them. Machines taking people's jobs and people having to adapt to new roles has happened throughout history. Digital is the next phase and is bringing this to more and more industries and helping them become more efficient.

There is some amazing footage on the internet of Ocado's distribution centre, with baskets of produce being delivered all over the place, all run entirely by computers. If you have not seen it, you should search for it now. It is mind blowing how everything gets to where it needs to be a lot more efficiently than when you have people doing the role.

Another good example of this is Receipt Bank. As a tool for you to use, it will save you time and money in dealing with expense claims. As a company, by using Machine Learning internally, they reduced the cost of processing a document from just over £1 to nearer 1p. Removing people from the process and investing in the right technology saves them hundreds of thousands of pounds a year in processing costs.

So, yes, the investment in technology may well mean you need fewer staff doing a particular role. In becoming more efficient, you may well have other functions that they can focus their time and effort on that have not yet become automated. You will have roles where the personal touch is more important, such as in customer service. It may well be the case that some of the new tools you introduce will allow them to upskill themselves. Just like reapers that learnt how to tend horses, they may find roles that enable them to flourish and help make your business become the efficiency machine that it needs to

"

You must find
your own
way and find
what works
for you.

be. Work with staff to ensure they benefit from digital and can see the opportunities it brings.

BENEFITS OF A DIGITAL CULTURE

What a lot of businesses are trying to do, and failing at, especially those that are already established, is to try and act like a digital start up. They see the news with the values being placed on these companies and then think that is how they should also behave. This is not the way to think of your business. For every digital start up that succeeds, there are hundreds that fail.

I have worked with companies that have implemented ways of working that large multinational software giants have used and then wondered why they have not had the same success. Some of these use things like the two-pizza analogy. Teams that are set up to deliver projects should be able to be fed with two pizzas. I think this is to limit it to about six people – although with my friends this team would be two people. But there are a small number of successes too.

You must find your own way and find what works for you. Look at what others are doing, but then adapt this to your business. You cannot instil the culture of Google into your business by telling everyone to be more like Google. It is not going to work. Your company culture and what works best for you will come from a bit of trial and error. Largely it will come down to the way that you communicate with your employees. This comes from the strategy that has come from clear engagement with them. Make them feel part of the journey and that they have a say in what happens. During the Discuss stage of the Be The Five methodology you will start to build relationships with your staff and use their knowledge to help you to define the problems that you are now trying to solve. Continue that journey with them as you begin to deliver projects and outcomes. A digital culture comes from a communication culture.

You will naturally build a company culture off the back of this. You cannot just stick a bowl of fruit at the front and a ping pong table at the back and tell people you have a good culture. Through the proper planning and engagement of all employees throughout your digital projects you will find that they become more interested and more involved in these projects. They will also start to Discuss and Discover digital tools themselves and offer better feedback and improvements. If you can harness this communication culture in your staff, you will always be looking forwards and working in unity to deliver the most efficient business to your customers. If you do not include employees, then you will see the opposite reaction and they will drag their heels on digital projects.

1. Digital changes the working day

One of the key things you can consider with digital is working hours. I have a personal dislike of the fact that a company basically owns you for a set number of hours per week, but this is the culture we have grown up with.

This 9 to 5, 40-hour working week culture is ingrained in society.

People trudge into the office to do a set number of daily hours. They are looked at suspiciously if they leave five minutes before 5pm. In today's digital world this is absolute nonsense. During the COVID-19 pandemic, I had never before seen so many photos on social media of people discovering online meetings. It is like it was the first time anyone had worked from home. I first worked from home, three days a week, 20 years ago. The fact that this is still novel to some is embarrassing. There are some jobs where being in an office or having set hours is a must. For the vast majority this is not the case, as we have seen all over the world.

There have been two big problems with the move to working from home for most people. The first was that they were still acting as if they were in the office. The number of meetings they had was the same as it was in the office. The novelty of seeing a colleague on a screen was a big thing. Zoom meetings were filling diaries as people craved human interaction. Zoom fatigue became a thing. Rather than worry about how you do the meeting, you need to consider whether the meeting was even required. The first thing you can do is to start to cull a whole host of these meetings from your diaries. They are not relevant in today's world, with all the digital collaboration tools available. Yes, some are essential and will always be. A lot are time fillers due to the number of hours people must work to fulfil their employment contracts. We have all sat through pointless meetings so let us not pretend that they are all essential. Cull that diary and make better use of other digital collaboration tools that allow you to share information as and when it suits you best.

The second problem, and the most important one, is the hours worked. Staff should not be owned for a set number of hours a week. This misconception comes from this historic 9 to 5 office day and ends up with staff being very inefficient. Hanging around until going home time. Speaking to colleagues about irrelevant issues. Doing tasks inefficiently or sending pointless emails. Having long tea breaks. Having irrelevant meetings and generally finding things to do. The one thing we should have learnt by now is that, to manage your staff effectively in a digital world, they should be salaried on an outcome basis and not an hours basis.

As an example, I'm commissioned to write a digital strategy for you, and you tell me that it must be on your desk by the 15th of the month. If I deliver it on the 15th of the month, then how I got there should be no real concern of yours. I may work two hours in the morning, two in the afternoon and three at night. I might work from 2pm to 10pm, it is completely irrelevant to you. Unfortunately, too many managers still view productivity and efficiency as the number of hours someone works. This is down to poor management skills. It also leads to inefficient processes not improving as people need to fill their days. You need to be able to set your staff a series of outcomes and

73

timescales and then let them be free to deliver. Are you paying someone £30,000 a year to deliver outcomes or to turn up for a set number of hours? How do you even know what the right number of hours is?

2. Digital helps the environment

Digital tools and internet connectivity mean that we can be much more flexible as a workforce. Not only will this help your company and your culture, but it will also help the environment. As the COVID-19 lockdown showed, nature has a way of recovering when people are largely removed from the equation. The waters of Venice became clear. Pollution in China and Italy dropped. The Himalayas were visible from India for the first time in decades and there were many more examples of this. Vehicles were removed from the roads in the UK and air quality improved. There is no reason why we cannot continue that trend forever and with digital you can offer your staff real flexibility over how they work, when they work and where they work. Allow them to make the decisions that suit them best but still deliver maximum efficiency for your business.

Learning how to manage your employees from an outcome perspective and not a time perspective will provide huge benefits to your employees, your business, and the environment. For you this will become simple, due to the work you will undertake around outcomes and desired outcomes. These should be very familiar phrases with your staff, making it easy to move to and manage an outcome model.

I once deployed a series of laptops to a team of staff that were going to trial homeworking. Their manager asked me what software I was installing on the laptop. I replied with the team's standard software set up. To be told, 'No, that is not what I meant. I meant what software, so I know they are working.' I immediately knew the project was going to be a failure. The technology would inevitably get blamed, as it always does. The manager still thinking that the staff doing their 35 hours at home was all that mattered. At no point had they considered managing by outcomes.

Under normal circumstances, the likelihood is that your staff will be more efficient at home. With fewer distractions they can probably do eight hours' work in five hours. Let them finish once they have completed their tasks. There will be other weeks or days where they need to work ten hours to complete their outcomes. You need to trust them to manage their own work. Offer them support to do this. I have worked with plenty of people who can be in an office for seven hours and do nothing at all. I have been in offices where staff have five meetings back to back and then go home. I have been in offices where staff spend seven hours sending emails to other staff asking them to do things and not achieve anything themselves. You will be well on your way to having the digital tools to make your business as efficient as possible. Step up and help your workforce become as efficient as they need to be. Allow more working from home or from the office, if they choose. Allow them to choose when to work (in most cases), even if they are office based. Work to outcomes not a set number of hours. From this, the culture of your organisation will develop further and help you build a successful business with an amazing culture.

3. Digital enables freedom

That's a bold claim but think about it for a minute. If we can reduce travel and give colleagues more flexibility over their hours and locations, then we are giving them freedom. Freedom to choose how, where and when to work. Sitting behind this enablement are digital tools. We all saw how video conferences took off during the COVID-19 pandemic. It was the main headline for a lot of the period. Behind that, though, we have users who have moved to G Suite or Office 365. Suddenly emails and documents are available 24/7 over an internet connection. Companies like Slack, a collaboration tool, saw demand increase to far higher levels and far more quickly than it ever had before. Giving users these digital tools to stay connected, communicate, and access the right information was vital in keeping staff in touch and effective.

No longer were they limited by systems only being available 9-5 and then unavailable due to upgrades overnight. We have all had days where the systems we need to use are unavailable. It's incredibly annoying. I know many companies who run overnight processes on their systems and, as such, they are then unavailable for staff to use. In today's world that doesn't have to be the case.

Having systems that are available 24/7. Systems that

allow communication, allow collaboration, allow con-sistency will all allow your staff to have more freedom to work in the way that suits them best. If they have this freedom of choice, then they will be more efficient and effective for your business.

I'm a night owl. I'm pretty useless in the mornings. If I have to get up, then it takes me a good few hours of tea drinking and procrastination before I'm up to speed. In the afternoon I work quickly and efficiently and will happily work later into the evening. I have that choice. Most of the companies I work with use Slack. I can catch up on any-thing in my own time and have the freedom that I enjoy. I get all my emails to my phone. I can read them in my own time. I can choose which to reply to and when. Anything less formal and related to a project goes into the Slack channel to be picked up by the right person or team.

I can do my banking online or from my phone. I can pay invoices from my phone. That gives me the freedom to do it from anywhere at any time. It also gives my cus-tomers the option to contact or buy me at any time too.

Digital technology really can give you freedom. It gives us the freedom to communicate via a variety of methods. It gives us the freedom to collaborate. It gives us the freedom to work the hours that suit us. It gives us the freedom to work from anywhere. It's about choice. Are you giving your colleagues the freedom they want or need? Are you getting the best from your staff? Digital allows you to think differently. Free yourself from legacy practices.

4. Digital brings you closer

It is ironic that the same technology that can help you be more flexible with work location and hours worked can also bring you closer. It can bring you closer as a team through digital collaboration tools, instant messaging over emails, chat spaces, and video communication. Being a remote worker used to mean just that. You were remote. You may get a phone call or an email, but it was unlikely that you were fully engaged or collaborative. Today it's fully inclusive.

Video conferencing has made the world a much smaller place. Remote work today does not just mean working from home. Remote work means that you can be anywhere in the world, as long as you have an internet connection. I have been to Singapore and Sydney on a six-day trip without needing to take a day off work. I worked the hours I needed to, kept on top of all my work and was available to all of the team that I managed. Yes, there were time differences but only one person in the company twigged that I was away, and I think they were told. Now you do not need to be as sneaky as me, because there is no need to be. I chose to go away and to work at the same time and it made very little difference to my productivity. As I have said, I work different hours anyway, so it was quite normal for me and my team to communicate at odd hours.

The point is that, as much as we like to think of roles being location based, they really are not anymore. There is no reason why I could not work in the UK and live in the Middle East or vice versa. If you are at home anyway, and communicating by video conference, then exactly where you are makes no difference. There may be times when you need to be awake at an odd hour, but they are few and far between.

It is the collaboration tools that are now available that really bring you closer, wherever you are in the world. We can Facetime with relatives in Australia or New Zealand. I often chat on LinkedIn to people in America. I have connections from all over the world that I would never have connected with otherwise.

Your teams may use tools to bring them closer as a team, or they may use tools to bring them virtually closer. How and why you use them will be to the benefit of your business. You can think on a global scale. Or you can keep it local. Ensuring that you have the right tools will mean that, whatever you decide, your employees can still feel close.

Why 95%
Get it Wrong

INTRODUCTION

The entrepreneur and founder of Dent Global, Daniel Priestley, tweeted on the 16th December 2019:

'Going into the 2020s you want to get at least a basic knowledge of:

- ○ 5G
- ○ AI
- ○ Quantum Computers
- ○ Sensors

○ IoT

○ **Blockchain'**

The tweet was aimed at the entrepreneurs he was working with. However, it is relevant to anyone in business. It highlights the biggest issue in digital without really meaning to. The reason so many projects fail is that they are IT projects. And people outside of IT are not interested in IT and do not understand it. They often feel that it is being forced on them before they are ready. They do not understand the benefits, because they are not explained properly in non-technical language. IT is not their job and they make it clear that they do not want to know.

Within three months of writing this tweet the world changed forever with the COVID-19 pandemic and the very rapid shift to remote working. Suddenly IT teams were forced to put in place systems to enable staff to work from home. These were systems that should have been in place a decade before. Jobs that could not be performed from home were now being performed remotely on a large scale. The valuation of Zoom went sky high and, for a time, became a novelty. However, what this did show was that too much of IT and technology is reactionary to situations and largely ignored in the main. It is the same as IT failures: your system may work 29 days out of 30, but you will remember the one day it did not work.

Well, it is now time for that to change. It's the 2020s, as a business leader you can no longer afford to ignore technology and leave it up to others. It is now the time for you to step up.

The mistake made by many leaders is that they assume that IT will cover all these bases for the business. However, IT does not always understand the needs of the business and will continue to deliver the best IT for IT. Therefore, it is now fundamental that businesses and leaders have a certain level of understanding of digital and the various topics covered by the generic term. Then they will better understand how these can benefit the business and how to ensure that projects deliver successful outcomes. Far too often, digital projects fail to add business value. A quick Google search on 'digital transformation failure rates' will bring back some staggering numbers.

For digital transformation, research suggests that only 5% of projects meet or exceed expectations. That is a ridiculously low figure. It means that 95% of projects fail to deliver business value. Depending on the website you visit, you may get a slightly higher figure; I have seen success rates at up to 20%, but that is about as high as it ever gets. So, on the one hand, you have an award-winning entrepreneur tweeting that technology is vitally important to your business and then, on the other, multiple websites stating that the success rates of these programmes is as low as 5%. Not only can you view failure by the costs involved, but also the reputational damage. We have all seen news items on large-scale IT problems and the damage that brings to businesses. You cannot afford to fail in either aspect.

WHAT IS GOING WRONG?

Let us start with what Daniel is actually saying. He is not saying that you need to understand how these technologies are built and how they work. He is saying that you need to understand what they are and how your business can use them. From there, you need to be able to put together a strategy that delivers business benefits and then show you can deliver against it with tangible outcomes.

Understanding how technology can be used is obviously going to be beneficial for your business but this brings me onto the single biggest thing that needs to be addressed before you even start looking at technology. This is something that the industry has been peddling for years and has become the norm for all work in digital. It is a phrase that is used all the time and has even managed to change its meaning over time. I have even used it myself in this book. The phrase in question is 'digital transformation', and it is a phrase that needs to be killed off sooner rather than later. Here is a true story to give you some context:

> *Once upon a time, sat on a lovely green leaf at the bottom of your garden was a little caterpillar. He was happily munching away, filling his belly with leaves, slowly making his way around the plant.*
>
> *A second caterpillar slowly wandered over and said, 'Are you ready to transform into a butterfly?'*
>
> *'Why would I want to do that?' he asked. 'I'm quite*

happy being a caterpillar, although I do move quite slowly.'

'Being a butterfly will be amazing, though. You won't even recognise yourself. In fact, no-one will even know you used to be a caterpillar.'

'But I don't want to transform into a butterfly and have no-one recognise me. I just want to be a faster caterpillar!'

Obviously, this isn't a true story, but this is the problem with transformation: most companies do not need to transform or to change into something unrecognisable from what they were before. Society has historically led us to believe that we want to become the butterfly. We want to emerge transformed into a beautiful, winged creature. The trouble with butterflies is that they die. They die quite quickly in most cases. The same is true of transformation programmes. They too die. The change is too big and too widespread for it to fully take hold and be implemented across a business. Yet we still cling to the societal norm of becoming a butterfly. I've shown you the failure rates already. It is fine for your company to be a caterpillar. You do not need to undergo this dramatic transformation to a butterfly. You need to become better and more efficient at being a caterpillar. You do not need to dramatically change. You need small incremental improvements.

You can do this through utilising the correct digital tools and focusing on delivering business benefits. Not all historical analogies are correct today!

The reason so many transformations fail is that they are trying to achieve something that they do not need to achieve. In fact, the industry has caught onto this level of failure and now the marketeers have started quoting phrases like 'digital transformation is not about the technology, it is about the people and culture' or other such nonsense. It is trying to move the narrative away from their software not delivering, or the projects people are working on failing, to another message on people and culture failure. There are hundreds of definitions out there and the more recent ones always come back to people, process, and culture. But you don't need to start with transformation. Forget about it.

For the rest of this book, we are not going to talk about the transformation of your business. Your business is probably fine as it is. If you run a plumbing company, you will still do plumbing. If you run an accountancy firm, you will still do accounting. You are not changing from a caterpillar to a butterfly. You are going to be a more efficient caterpillar. If every company that said it was transforming actually transformed, we would live in a very confused world. If no-one told you a caterpillar transforms into a butterfly, you would think they were two completely different species. Your business will stay the same business, you will just be more efficient and more effective at what you do.

Back to those failure rates, you would think for an industry so sure of itself and with so many expert voices, and even more voices with opinions, that success rates would be much higher. If you visit LinkedIn or Twitter you will find experts in all shapes and sizes guaranteeing you digital transformation and plenty of advice, but still it is going wrong somewhere. So, what is happening?

LEADERS LACK DIGITAL SKILLS

The right starting point for digital programmes is the fact you should be thinking efficiency over transformation. This automatically changes the mindset of what you are trying to achieve.

The second point comes down to knowledge of digital. In the opening chapters, I talked about my work at Peterborough City Council. Outwardly, things were going great for me. As I said, I was being invited to speak at conferences, was having videos made, interviews were forthcoming, and I was on a high. Someone who a few years earlier could barely turn on a computer was being lauded as a leader in digital. I believe that a lot of it was down to the fact that I did not have a background in IT. I therefore had not limited myself to my own knowledge, or lack of it. I had the business knowledge to see how things needed to change. I could challenge people on why tasks were being undertaken in one way and not another.

I also have a background in sport and was always captain or vice-captain of teams and a natural leader on the pitch. I was not afraid of standing up and being controversial or putting my head above the parapet. I have always questioned decisions to improve. I may have initially been terrified of public speaking, but that was more around the thought of being found out than the actual speaking. In a changing room before a game it was all I would do.

Inwardly, the cracks were starting to appear in some of the programmes of work. A few conversations with the right people and it soon became very clear why.

After I had written the strategy, it had to go through two levels of approval to become an official council strategy. The first level was the Corporate Management Team, made up of the Senior Directors and Chief Executive. The second was through a cabinet made up of the most senior councillors at the council. Being slightly naïve, I was overjoyed when the strategy passed through relatively easily with no major issues, complaints, or difficult questions at either meeting. It had been approved. Everyone was happy. We were moving forwards. But no-one had read it either.

Ok, maybe a couple of them had. But they had not understood it. Although it was a very modern cloud strategy, at its heart it was very much about using a single platform across all services. This would join the data up and offer greater insight into the residents of the city and therefore deliver more efficient services. With the platform of choice there was also an ecosystem of products that would help remote working, give more resilience, and allow staff to use their device of choice. The main benefit was also that the platform was flexible enough to be programmed to suit new processes and not be as rigid as the legacy systems. If the legacy system said the process was ABC then it had to be ABC, we needed tools that could be BCA or CBA. Now they were finally getting that, and the service could choose how it wanted to deliver the service. Not how the software company said it should be delivered.

However, the business analysts assigned to the project were moved on. Restructures that were meant to happen did not. Building some of the new systems was left to single resources and it started to unravel. The implications of the strategy, and how it was going to help enable the wider service delivery programme that the council had, were not understood at all. It was also a five-year strategy. It was a five-year strategy because it needed to be that long. There would be ups and downs along the way, with wins constantly being delivered, but to get to the desired end point was a long journey. This was a key point that I thought had been understood, but it clearly had not been.

We were left with a service delivery programme that was constantly changing and a technology strategy that was not understood. It was left to one person to deliver and in a much-shortened timeframe. It was clear that it was being looked at as a technology-led programme, which it was not. It never should be and approaching it in this manner was an element of why these programmes generally fail. The digital aspect of any business is to make the business better at what it does, not to lead the way and change the way the business works. That is the leader's job.

I have publicly stated that your CIO (Chief Information Officer / Head of IT) is often the worst person to lead these programmes of work. It is not necessarily their fault. To truly embed new technology and new ways of delivering a service takes a different skill set than that of a technical CIO role. It also puts staff off because, as soon as they think something is an IT project, they become disinterested and assume it is not their job. Going back to Daniel's tweet at the start of this chapter, everybody needs to start getting an understanding of technology and how it can best be used to deliver your business outcomes. You need to be helping your staff to see the benefits that adopting new digital tools will give them. You can only do this if you understand them.

Key to any programme of work delivering results is leadership. Those organisations that have strong leadership with an understanding of the subject matter will have a far higher success rate than those that do not. Leaders of the future will need the knowledge of technology and how it can shape their business or disrupt their industry. In reading this book, you are taking the first crucial steps towards giving your business the best chance to succeed. As I have said, you do not necessarily need to know how the technology works, as far as you are concerned it could be magic. You do need to understand the benefits of technology to your business and, more importantly, you need to be able to speak to your IT department. Whether in house or outsourced, you need to find a common language and to be able to challenge their thoughts and ideas on how the business needs to use technology.

NOT UNDERSTANDING HOW TO USE TECHNOLOGY

One of the main failures within digital programmes is buying new technology when you already have the tools available to complete the job required. Do you know what you already have, and are you using it to its full potential? I have often heard people say how good they are at Excel. To them, being good on Excel is being able to do a pivot table. When you start asking them about 'V' or 'H' lookups they go completely blank. Yet this is a basic task when you consider the overall power of Excel. Most of us barely scratch the surface. Looking at your current tools and finding out if you are using them efficiently is a crucial step and negates the need, in some cases, to go to market to buy new tools. Dig a little deeper into what you already have and explore the full functionality of it before you consider anything new.

Additionally, you may want to explore tools designed to work with your system. One of the most basic of these is something like a plug-in for Wordpress or G Suite. There are lots of app stores out there selling add-ons to improve and complement your current tools. Take time to explore these as you might save yourself the expense of a new project.

Once you have explored what you have and whether you are utilising it effectively, you can start to look elsewhere and plan the future state. Too many projects try to fix problems that do not exist by buying new technology.

A lot of the time the tools you already have can achieve the same outcome.

Do not be scared of digital; there is very little out there that is not just a new way of doing an old manual process. The opportunity you have here is twofold. Firstly, you can review your processes to be more efficient, which may not require new technology or, in fact, any technology. Secondly, you then have the opportunity to automate those inefficient manual processes with RPA (Robotic Process Automation). RPA has been happening for hundreds of years in some form. Taking a manual process and automating it. The best example, which I've mentioned before, is the combine harvester. Years ago, we sent people out into fields to cut down and collect hay. Then a machine was invented that could do this work for them, removing the need for most manual intervention. Over time, combines have improved and improved and no doubt, in the future, will soon also come with artificial intelligence and self-driving. The point is that we have been using machines and robots to do tasks since before the Industrial Revolution. Digital is just the next step in this. Someone who says they cannot understand digital is saying they do not understand how a combine harvester has replaced a field of humans. There are plenty of opportunities to look at processes across your business and improve them. You will also be able to see how automating some manual processes will help you become more efficient.

POOR DIGITAL STRATEGIES

All too often, I see digital or technology strategies that are full of IT jargon and deliver no benefits to the business. They often deliver benefits to the IT department but that is not the point of IT. IT is a service that is there to give you the best possible chance to succeed as a business. This is often overlooked and forgotten because no-one outside of IT really knows what they do. It is all too easy to have a number of acronyms thrown at you, alongside some technical jargon, and for you to walk away none the wiser. Likewise, IT themselves must get better at speaking to the business and understanding business needs. By improving your knowledge of technology, you will also be able to help IT to understand the business needs.

Let me give you an example of this using cloud computing. Now you might not know what cloud computing is. You might not really care. I can guarantee you that most of your staff will not care about whether their software is cloud or not. What they want is a system that works and allows them to do their job and to do their job well. No-one likes to use inefficient or unreliable software that constantly crashes. It costs time and money to have that. For me, as someone who works in digital, then yes, I do care. I care because cloud computing gives me the tools I need to be able to do my job better (or more efficiently). And that is really the point here. IT is a support service that has a role to ensure that the end users have the right tools to do their job in the most efficient and effective manner. Too often the focus is on the IT department and cloud first strategies, whereas the strategy must be about the end users first. The trend has been for IT to write a strategy that focuses on cloud technology. You may well have heard of 'Cloud First' strategies that government departments have launched. This, though, is the wrong approach. IT strategies need to be user and business first.

To 90% of end users the fact that the technology we all use every day and take for granted is cloud based is in the main entirely irrelevant. Does anyone using Instagram or Facebook care that much that it is cloud based? What really matters to them is that they can post an image or text or read / see images and text from others. As long as the application they are working on or using at the time opens and lets them do what they need to do in a timely manner then there is generally very little interest in the technology that sits behind it.

The same is true of most staff that I come across in businesses. What they want is an application that opens and works when they need it to, allows them to complete their work in the most efficient manner and is reliable. That may be cloud, hybrid or on-premise. You do not need to worry about these terms. They are just different methods of delivering software to you. You need to worry about ensuring you have the right tools.

At school I played rugby. I was quite good, or I thought I was. I look back now, though, and think that, although I could run, pass, and kick, I had no idea about the theory of the game. We used to run drills all the time, but no-one

Once you
have the
basics the rest
will start to
make sense.

ever took the time to sit me down and explain why or what we were trying to achieve from them. With this knowledge, the level to which I played would have been increased massively. I had all the tools but no idea what I was really doing with them. With digital it worked the other way; I understood the theory first. I saw how it could be used to improve services, how you can play the game better, and then I implemented the changes. The same is now true of you. Taking the first step in reading this book will help put you in a place where you understand the theory and have the basic knowledge to really press on and implement digital tools that make you a game winner.

What leaders need to be looking at is the benefits of their technology to the end user and not just the benefits of their technology to the IT department. The benefits to IT are, of course, important, but secondary to the end users, whether that be customers or staff.

The key section of the Be The Five methodology is Decide. This is where we set your digital strategy. It is this that will give you the advantage to improve your business. It is the single thing that will bring your company together to deliver real beneficial improvements to the services you deliver, both internally and externally. In following the methodology, you will play a crucial role in approving the strategy in a way that you understand the benefits but without the need for technical jargon. You will be looking for clear business benefits that meet your business goals and measurable outcomes. A poor digital strategy is the downfall of many programmes of work.

You can waste hundreds of thousands of pounds trying to implement the wrong technology with the wrong strategy. I have seen millions spent on new finance systems to find that staff do not like the process and have started using more spreadsheets. I have seen months spent trying to implement new systems without the business benefits being understood. Teams that were disengaged and not onboard increased the delays, eventually abandoning the project before it went live. Whilst the strategy is key, circulating it, understanding it, approving it, including everyone, and communicating it are also key. If you miss the 'what is in it for me?', you will miss the benefits.

BE THE FIVE

Taking these first steps in digital can be daunting. We have built a secluded industry. One for the nerds. The guys who hide in the basement. A perception that is perpetuated by programmes like *The IT Crowd*. We talk in acronyms and jargon. We think technology will solve everything. We ask you to turn it off and on again. We play Warhammer at night. We are scared of daylight. We do not wash. We are introverts. We are not like you.

Well, some of those are true and some are not. It can be daunting, yes. There is nothing to fear, though. Digital and the benefits it can bring your business can be straightforward. The methodology you will learn in this book will walk you through the steps you need to take. Yes, there is a lot to take on board. There are new ways of working.

New ideas. New technologies. There are over 1,500 different marketing solutions currently on the market. How do you choose the right one? The same is true of other systems.

But you will get there. Once you have the basics the rest will start to make sense. I will guide you through the different steps. There is no little pill that you can take to magically understand it. You are going to have to go and do some research. You are not alone, though. You will get there. You will become part of the 5% that do deliver. I will show you how. And we will do it together.

For more information please visit: **www.bethefive.co.uk.**

4

Digital Myth Busting

There are countless myths and misconceptions that business leaders have on digital. I have listed some of the main ones here that I have most frequently come across. These myths can cause many blockers before you have even tried to implement any digital. They cause more issues than they solve. Often, they are perpetuated by people that do not want to change. Or marketing spiel by companies preying on insecurities. They are huge blockers to positive change. Let me unravel some of these and explain why you can ignore them. Breaking through these will help you to understand how digital can help you and how you can utilise the internet to deliver better, more efficient, and more effective services.

MYTH 1: DIGITAL IS ABOUT TRANSFORMATION

Often when people think digital, they immediately think about social media and marketing. To keep it simple throughout this book we are going to be talking about using tools that utilise the internet. For the purposes of this book, and simplifying terminology, we are going to treat cloud computing and digital as the same thing. Think cloud services, internet, mobile phones, tablets, social media, apps, internet of things. All are digital services. It is about using the internet (wi-fi and 3/4/5G included) to collect, transfer, share, view and use data.

There are lots of digital definitions out there. Some descriptions add in that digital is a way of working and all sorts but let us just stick with utilising the internet to deliver services, either internally or to customers. As we have stated, you do not need to know all the specifics and idiosyncrasies of technology.

So, what about those companies that have digitally transformed or, more accurately, been held up as beacons of digital transformation? Well, dig a little deeper and the majority have not. Let us start with the two main ones that are always used as examples of transformation, Uber and Netflix. How have they used digital to use data more efficiently?

Netflix, for those that remember, sent DVDs through the post, in fact they still do, but most people are unaware of that. With the improvement of internet speeds and device capability, it was clear that it would be more efficient to deliver content (data) via the internet, instead of through the post. Subscribers have access to a wider range of content that can be consumed more quickly via the internet than it could through a DVD postal subscription. By looking at more efficient ways of delivering content via digital tools, Netflix helped to transform their industry. Significantly, they did not transform themselves away from a company that provides movies and films. The Netflix brand is still related to the earliest version of the company. A subscription content company and that element of the company is still fully recognisable today.

So here the consequence of Netflix looking to become more digitally efficient was that the industry was transformed, and now the way we consume content has changed forever. There are more players in the market and more content is being produced exclusively by these providers. However, they did not set out to transform the industry, that was secondary. Netflix just became a faster caterpillar.

Ok, but Uber surely did digital transformation? Again, no. Partly because they did not exist in any other form previously and partly because their model is based around efficiency. In this instance the efficiency is not aimed at the company itself, but its customers. In this particular instance, 'customers' covers both drivers and those

wanting a ride. What Uber did was give users a more efficient way of hailing a cab. No more standing in the street
waving an arm, not knowing if the light on means free or
busy, hoping that a free taxi sees you and stops. Waving
an arm is an analogue data transfer.

You then had to make sure you had the correct money
on you, without knowing what the fare was going to be,
unless it was a regular journey. Uber took that experience
and gave you a digital app that hailed a ride as soon as
you wanted one. It even gave you tracking so you knew
when the Uber car was arriving. The registration number,
the driver's name, and the price. At the end of the journey,
the money is simply debited from your account, without
you scrambling around for cash... or, what has probably
happened to all of us, having to stop the journey halfway
to visit a cash point. Uber has given us a much more efficient way of using taxis through digital and the internet.
The days of phoning the taxi firm to ask how long your
car will be only to be told that it is just around the corner
are gone.

For Uber drivers, it also gives them a more efficient
way of choosing jobs to take and knowing exactly where
those jobs are without sitting in taxi ranks or driving around
the streets hoping to be flagged down. Taxis hailed in this
way also have very little choice on end destination and
mostly accept any fare that hops in the back.

Whether you like Uber or not, the digital experience it
gives users is more efficient than a traditional taxi firm and
hence why it has taken off around the world so quickly. If

the traditional taxi service itself had become more efficient for customers, then Uber would not exist. So yes, it has transformed the taxi industry, but it has done this by looking at the most digitally efficient way to deliver a service making its customers faster caterpillars.

What you will notice in both of these examples is that both Uber and Netflix have given a more efficient service to their customers through using their own devices. With Uber, users require a smartphone with 4/5G and with Netflix they need their own internet connection. They have made the customer more efficient in allowing them to (or making them) use their own tools. And the customers are happy to do this.

Let us also now consider the fast food giant McDonald's. Not something you would generally associate with digital, but they too have been using digital tools to become more efficient. In this instance it is around reducing waste. Previously, food was very much cooked in bulk with one person estimating how much to cook at one time. It was then wrapped or packaged and kept in a food warmer behind the staff working the tills and serving customers. You would queue up and be served by the person behind the till. The cooked food could be kept in the warmer for a certain length of time. Once it had passed its time freshness limit it was thrown in the bin. At the end of the day, the waste bin was emptied and counted. This was then matched against items sold and stock levels. The level of waste was quite high, as there was no way of determining exactly how much to cook of each food type.

Fast forward to today and in most McDonald's, you can now order via a large digital touch screen self-service kiosk. This has several efficiencies. Ordering queues are reduced and users can take their time and do not feel rushed once they get to the counter. McDonald's have fewer staff serving. More importantly, McDonald's can move to a cook to order model that reduces the amount of waste they are producing, increasing the efficiency of the restaurant, and making it more profitable. In making themselves more efficient, they have also improved the customer experience. In this example you are still using screens owned by McDonald's in place of your phone, but that will be the next step. Making your customers more efficient in consuming your service is a key element of successful digital projects.

MYTH 2: THE CLOUD IS JUST FOR IT

Just moving services and processes to digital is largely pointless without an understanding of where the efficiency is going to be delivered from. Where the cloud comes into its own is the ability to be configured in a way to enable and support business efficiency in a relatively speedy process. This is often without huge upfront costs and undertaken in an iterative manner where the only real requirement is access to the internet. Companies that are not looking at the cloud will fall behind those that are. The reason for moving to the cloud, though, is for its business benefits and not the IT benefits.

Cloud computing, of course, has huge positives from an IT perspective. These include free upgrades and improvements, 24x7 access, security, flexibility, per user per month (pupm) pricing model, and being mobile ready and infrastructure free. Cloud also provides everyday tools, such as instant messaging, FaceTime, ubiquitous access, configurable systems, collaboration tools and an ecosystem of products that focus on the end user and can help change the way users work.

Look at how workers adapted to remote working and video conferencing during the COVID pandemic. Although this was forced, it broke many myths about home or remote working. All enabled by the internet and cloud.

Whilst there are clearly IT related benefits of cloud computing, we already know that that is not the focus. The focus is the end users.

As an example, let's consider your staff, maybe a salesperson, or an accountant. Do you think they care that their software is cloud hosted? Or do they want a system that works on a Monday morning? Something that allows them and their team to work efficiently, maybe from out of the office? Something that isn't subject to large amounts of downtime for power failures or essential maintenance or upgrades?

To the end user, the fact that the system that can provide all these things may well be cloud based is irrelevant to the fact that it just provides them. End users should not be looking for cloud first systems. They should be looking for systems that meet their requirements as end users. And as end users in today's world, these requirements should be very demanding. The fact that it is likely that only cloud solutions can or should be able to meet their demands is not the driver behind their decisions and nor should it be. And neither should IT costs.

The focus must be on the users of systems and away from IT's cloud first strategies. Of course, have cloud as the preferred option, it is still the right direction to go in, in the main, but temper it with the needs of the end user. Use the cloud technology to enable your business plans but establish these plans first. With the tools available to users these days, there really is very little to limit the art of the possible. Cloud first plans will lose the interest of the users. Focus on users first and then work back to the technology.

MYTH 3: IT IS TOO EXPENSIVE

IT costs are an important part of any plans that you may have for your business, but they should not be the driving force for change. I once read a report, 5 or 6 years ago now, that a prominent CIO had written explaining that he had undertaken a study and concluded that cloud computing was more expensive than on premise computing. Therefore, he would be continuing as is, managing the IT estate himself.

The problem with this was twofold. Firstly, yes cloud is not always cheaper than on premise – that is a given. If you have already spent money and accounted for costs and resources then moving systems away from hardware you own that is now essentially free to use and depreciating will cost more. It is also generally a pay per usage model and therefore costs can spiral if they are not controlled. The report also failed to mention all the benefits of the cloud and their current time spent on upgrading and patching systems, downtime due to failures and staff costs, and many other important time and efficiency savings.

However, the main reason the report was irrelevant was because it was looking purely at how much IT costs the business and not how much IT can benefit the business. Let us say you are a medium-sized company and you spend £100,000 a year on your IT. If you have told your IT manager to cut the IT budget by 10% then he is going to be removing systems, sweating assets, and looking for the cheapest solutions, not the best solutions. You may have saved £10,000 but you may also have given inefficient tools to your workforce. You have made life harder for salespeople to sell. Made it harder for accountants to do the books. Restricted workers to being office based. You now suffer from older equipment that fails regularly. You may well have cost the company a lot more than £10,000 but you have an IT manager who believes they have done a good job because they have hit their target.

Now let us say we increased the budget by £20,000 but, in doing so, we made your sales team more efficient. They had better data on your prospects and could speak to more each day. They could complete their tasks remotely and could choose to work more flexible hours with systems available 24/7. They ultimately sell more. Your accountants now have the right information they need. You no longer require temporary support in that team. Your management information is now real time, allowing you to make quicker and more accurate decisions. Through doing this, we could be adding another £100,000 of value to your business in efficiency. So, as a net figure, you are still £80,000 better off. You may now also provide a better service to your customers which should, in turn, lead to improved satisfaction rates and the ability to retain more customers and add more value to the business.

Investing in the right technology for your end users is more important than investing in the right technology for IT. But clearly you must know what efficiencies you can deliver and what success then looks like.

MYTH 4: YOU DO NOT NEED A BUSINESS CASE

One of the key inhibitors to businesses investing in digital tools is often the cost of the tool when the return is not always visible. At least from a cash perspective. As I have re-iterated many times through this book, you are focusing on efficiency.

This might be the efficiency of how you deliver a service, efficiency of dealing with customers, growing efficiently, or just being more efficient as a business. There-fore, spending money on digital tools that you do not already own is surely going to cost additional money. Yes, absolutely it will. If you have never owned a tool before then it will invariably be a cost that has never been bud-geted for before. Where you are replacing one system with another then this is easier to assess. Where you are introducing new technology, it is not.

Let us look at the airline industry as an example here. They have invested heavily in moving from a largely paper-based industry to an online experience. They have achieved this in moving from issuing paper tickets, to print at home tickets, to an airline app. You can now download your boarding card onto your own phone.

They have cracked efficiency from two angles. Firstly, they have made the whole experience of flying with them more efficient for the customer. Who honestly thought they would be fooled into printing their own tickets at home? Would they use their own ink and their own paper and still be pleased the airline let them do it themselves? They have transferred all the work onto the customer!

Secondly, they have made themselves more efficient by reducing their paper, printing, and mailing costs and associated staff.

What is important to note in this example is that the paper, printing, and mailing costs probably are not costs covered by the airline's IT budget. This was not work undertaken to make the IT costs reduce. This was a broader look at costs across the business and looking

Digital
does not
always
need to be
large scale.

at how to use digital to become more efficient. Very rarely in looking at digital tools will you primarily be looking at reducing IT costs. The business case is essential in understanding where the efficiency, and therefore the return on investment, is coming from.

I have worked with a council that wanted to implement GoCardless. It is a very cheap payment online direct debit solution. The saving was against the time and effort it took the team to manage 36 spreadsheets. The cost saving wasn't necessarily financial. It was a simpler process that freed staff up to do more valuable work. There was less manual input and therefore less risk of mistakes being made. It was a small efficiency saving for a small cost. Digital does not always need to be large scale programmes. It is why we focus on efficiency and not transformation. It is finding these key efficiencies that will help you develop the right mindsets.

The business case will also help you to determine how much to spend on improvements. If you are spending £20,000 to make your sales team 10% more efficient and they are all billing £10,000 a month, then they will be improving by £1,000 per month. If you have five of them, then it will take four months to break even on your investment. This is not always an exact science, but it is an important step. I've seen some digital 'experts' claim that there should not be business cases for digital and it should be all about giving customers a greater experience. This is, of course, nonsense. You have to know the return.

If you took the above example and spent £100,000, then if the sales team still improved by 10% you are looking at 20 months to break even. These figures do not need to be exact, but you should have a ballpark and a maximum figure to be working to.

If you were to look at development costs for the development of new tools and each week costs you about £5,000, then you must be able to sit with your development team or partner and understand how big the benefit will be. This will tell you how many weeks will get you to the maximum efficiency for the right development cost. You are looking at improving your services, internally or externally, to give you a return.

If you can only afford nine weeks, then you need to focus on the maximum return from those weeks. You can always add a tenth later if you look at the value added by the work being completed in that extra week.

What you cannot do, though, is just let a development team run for 15 weeks without being able to see the value added.

Developers will continue to develop and improve until they are stopped as they do not necessarily get involved in conversations about finances and business cases. I have seen development builds continue and continue for little gain. This is prevalent when the staff are employed by the company. This is because the cost is an internal salary cost and not always looked at in the context of the project that they are working on. Some of these projects have spent millions of pounds before they have been halted. No real end result or benefit has been delivered and it is an element of why we see such high failure rates.

As you can see, having a business case, even a very small one, is essential in delivering digital projects. Always know that you are in all likelihood going to increase your spend in IT. Just do it efficiently and in a controlled manner and understand the outcomes and efficiencies. Business cases that you can understand and review, will give you the insight to make the best investments. No longer will you be baffled by the jargon.

MYTH 5: YOU CANNOT MEASURE DIGITAL SUCCESS

Digital programmes often fail because people do not understand what the measure of success is. A good example of this is channel shift and improving the website of councils. You may or may not have noticed the tendency for your local council to add services to an online account or portal. In local government there is a huge emphasis, and a lot of money spent, on improving websites over the last five years and providing 'my account' style portals, also known as 'we want to be like Amazon'. These projects often fail to deliver the promised savings, though, as they have not looked at where the cost is.

To explain, you need to use the Pareto principle. In a council area you can say that roughly 80% of residents are low need and 20% high need. Take myself, for example, I maybe contact my council only once a year, if that. The majority of residents will be the same, about 80% in this example, and we would be classified as the low-need group.

The same is true of cost, except that 80% of council spend goes on serving the 20% of high-need residents. Most of these high-need residents will likely be people who do not use the internet and would be deemed low internet use category. No amount of online accounts and e-forms will help cut the spend to this 20%.

If we took a round number of council spend of £1,000,000 then £800,000 is spent on serving 20% of residents and £200,000 is spent on serving 80% of residents. Yet it is the 80% low-need residents that most of the website improvements are aimed at, where you have only got £200,000 of spend to make savings from, and they need the least help.

Simply drawing the above out will show you why you need to understand exactly who you are targeting and why and ensure there are benefits to both customer and the business. In this instance, the councils are making benefits to a low-need, low-cost set of customers without making any internal savings. It is a one-way improvement and will not result in high savings, which is the aim of these types of projects.

In truth, most council websites could be awful, making you download and print all documents, having no online forms at all. It would make very little difference to the 80% of residents as they only contact their council once or twice a year. The money being spent by councils is being spent in the wrong areas with the view that digital will save them money. After all, the main reason for doing this is the austerity cuts that the government has pushed on them over the previous decade.

The savings must come from what sits behind these services. The website efficiencies should only be implemented if there is also back office efficiency too. Savings estimated to be attributed to website redevelopments or online accounts will not deliver the savings required on their own. This is a fact that is often missed.

The secret to success in implementing projects of this type is to deliver a service to your customer where they must do all the work. Done in such a way that they thank you for it whilst also, just as importantly, allowing you to save money through making your internal processes easier and cheaper. Having a clear strategy with business outcomes will help you define this.

Great examples of this are both banks and supermarkets. With supermarkets they have introduced self-serve checkouts and told you, the consumer, that it is for your ease, benefit and speed. There you are scanning your own items, placing them in the bagging area, paying and off you go. All for your benefit. Not the fact that supermarkets can now employ fewer people. They can put more tills in a smaller space so have more shelf space. Not the reduction in cash payments that need to be processed and other benefits that they get from it. If it was purely the customer that benefitted, then there would not be any self-service tills. Look at the new Amazon stores where there are not even tills. You walk in and help yourself to goods and they are automatically detected and debited from your account. Again, reducing staff numbers and administration costs.

The same is true of banking apps. Moving to online banking allowed you to view and print your statements at home, for your benefit apparently. Not to reduce their own print and mailing costs or so they would require fewer staff. Now there is a mobile app that you download your statements onto. Again, saving them time and costs but sold as your benefit. So likewise, websites and online accounts need to be sold for the benefit of the customer and genuinely make their life easier, but it also must add real value to your business too. And this is an element that is all too often missed. Delight your customers with your services but do it in a way that allows you to become more efficient too. Do not deliver digital services to your customers in a way that ends up ultimately costing you more. Work out why you are doing it first.

With these services, where they have been very good to customers in enabling them to self-serve, the same cannot always be said of their staff. I have seen the internal workings of a global airline company from a staff perspective. It is so inefficient that it is shocking. I could guarantee that if the CEO had to use the same tools then they would all be replaced very quickly. Do you know the systems your team are expected to use and the processes that they must follow?

Likewise, you should be thinking of your staff in the

same way. Ensuring that they have the right tools and processes to be efficient is a key element of any programme. Whenever we talk about customers of digital these are both external and internal.

By defining the internal savings of a project, regardless of whether these are IT savings, cash savings or time savings, you will help determine the measure of success of a project. Go into these projects knowing exactly what you want to achieve. Do not rebuild a website for the sake of rebuilding it. What are you now offering the customer that also makes your roles easier? And where is the internal saving or efficiency coming from?

MYTH 6: MINIMUM VIABLE PRODUCT ALLOWS US TO DO THE MINIMUM

A common method of developing systems within a small budget or time frame is to build what is known as a Minimum Viable Product or MVP. It might be something you have not come across before, but it is a term you will hear time and time again when looking at digital technology. Where this is a completely new application then MVP is a very good way of building. When it is replacing an older system then it will often result in failure. The MVP version will almost certainly need to contain all the features of the system being replaced and will be too costly.

However, too many people focus on the Minimum

aspect. The focus needs to be on the Viable aspect.

For an MVP you build a very basic system with just the bare essentials. A good visualisation of this, if you want to build something that you are going to use to propel yourself forwards, is to build a roller skate. You may then improve this to a skateboard. You may then improve this to a bicycle, to be improved to a motorbike, to be improved to a car. What you are not doing is building part of the car initially and then adding to it to build a full car. You are building a quick tool that helps move you forwards. Then one that helps you move forwards a bit more quickly and so on. You may never actually get as far as the car. You may find that you get as far as the bicycle and any financial benefit of moving to the motorbike is wiped out by the further cost of development. This is perfectly fine. You do not always need to end up with the car. You need to end up with something viable.

You may well return to the project at a later date and add more to it as technology or the industry you are in grows, changes, or develops. A quick business case at this time will again see if the investment in going from a motorbike to a car is worthwhile at that stage. You may have had to stop at motorbike purely because you simply could not afford to move to the car. This, again, is perfectly fine. You do not have to do everything at once or at the same time. You may benefit from letting staff have a go on the motorbike for a while as their feedback will help you build a better car. But, by improving incrementally, you can make small efficiencies at every step, even if you never fully get to the car. You can start small and grow.

Remember that you do not necessarily have to be adding new features. You can stop the project of a new system as it's complete enough to deliver your outcomes. You may want to spend time making the same system even more efficient or making it more stable. You will need to have the knowledge to know when to stop and when to continue.

And, because you will know how to measure success, your project will not be one that fails. Just ensure that the focus is on the viable element and not the minimum elements. Your staff will thank you for it. What is the smallest viable solution you can implement that brings the biggest benefits?

MYTH 7: DIGITAL IS NOT MY JOB

The final myth is the single most important one. It is the one thing that holds companies back more so than any other. The 'it's not my job' mentality. This is the one that breaks so many programmes of work.

So, let us be very clear on this.

Digital is everyone's job.

Every business is a digital business.

If you think you are not, then you are destined to fail. You may provide services on top of digital. You may have work that is not digital, however, the majority of your work depends on digital. Even if you are new to it, you will still be digital in some ways. I guarantee that 99% of people

"

Digital is everyone's job.

---

reading this book have a smartphone. That is digital. If you can instil this way of thinking across the whole business, then you will place yourself ahead of the pack. As much as an accountant wants to be an accountant, they will still have a foundation of digital tools. I guarantee they use Excel or an equivalent. Maybe Xero, maybe GoCardless. There will be digital systems in place.

A plumber will still be a plumber, but maybe he now has a CRM, a finance system, Calendly to book appointments, text message updates on his arrival time. An iPad with access to trade shops to buy or order parts whilst on a job. A sat nav to find the address of their next job more quickly.

The foundations of every business and every role are digital. Embrace it, learn it, understand it. Do not just see your tools as bits of software that you use. They need to be looked after and managed. They need to help make you better at what you do. Think of digital as your assistant. What can it help you to achieve? How can it make you more efficient at what you do?

Saying you do not do digital or do not understand digital is not good enough. We're in the 2020s. Digital is prevalent everywhere. Everyone must know it. Those that do not will be left behind. You are a leader. Stand up and be counted. Get on board and start your journey here.

PART

2

The Be The Five Method

INTRODUCTION TO PART 2

Now that we have discussed the importance of digital to your business and the common problems in implementing it, it is time to look at how you break the cycle of 'digital failure' and set your business up to succeed.

The Be The Five methodology is a simple and easy to follow process that takes you through the vital steps that you must take in order to gain maximum benefit from your investment in digital. It is a collaborative approach to understanding your business needs. I want you to be in the 5% of projects that add value, by following the five steps of the method.

To achieve success in digital efficiency, there are five key steps to follow. I have developed these over the last decade of working in digital. Some may seem obvious, but you would be amazed how often they are missed and often that is the reason digital projects fail. Just as important as the five steps are the order in which they are undertaken. It is no coincidence that the first four of the five steps are before you procure or roll-out any new software. There are some basics that you need to get in place and understand before you proceed. The idea behind this methodology was borne through my own work in not just leading IT but also in understanding the difficulties of implementing and going live with software. The public sector is littered with digital failure, but it is no worse than the private sector, just ask Hertz. It just gets more press. I speak to all industries and companies. I work closely with a lot of suppliers and see the same issues over and over again. I speak at conferences to all industries and enjoy comparing issues across sectors. These are not unique to one industry. They are commonplace. I have been customer and supplier. I have hit every block and snag there is. More often than not it comes down to a lack of understanding and a lack of communication.

Too many businesses dive straight into buying new tools without having undertaken the necessary pre-work to understand the why or to communicate the why. They leave colleagues behind and digital sits as a separate workstream; often one that is seen as a nuisance or a hindrance rather than for the positives it can bring. Those who are anti-technology have often had a bad experience or just have not got their head around why projects are being undertaken. We are here to solve that.

The methodology works at all levels. Although aimed at leaders, who need to have overall ownership of the work, the methodology filters down to all levels. As stated, digital is everyone's job. Taking yourself through the steps of Be The Five is a great start. Getting everyone to go through the steps is an even better start. You can easily adapt any of the steps to anyone at any level within your business. Digital plays and will play such a fundamental part in the businesses of the future that it is imperative that everyone starts understanding it. Take the whole business on the journey with you.

The old saying of 'do not run before you can walk' stands true here. Digital teams are often guilty of embarking on projects on their own. Leaving the business and the employees behind and chasing the next shiny toy. If you do not understand digital or, in fact, what your IT or digital team are working on, and you have approved a strategy that you do not understand then you are setting yourself up for failure. It may be time to reign your team in and take a step back and ensure that the whole business is on the same journey. There really is no replacement for spending the time upfront ensuring that you are in the right place to deliver. Too often businesses want immediate results, but they do not actually know what these are. So, slow it down. Plan everything out properly. Follow the process and you will succeed.

Although each step is as crucial as the next, step three is really what is going to help your business become the efficiency engine that it needs to be. This step is all about your digital strategy. Getting this right will make life much easier for you in the long run. I will explain why this step is the most crucial when you get to it. However, you cannot get it right without steps 1 and 2 first, so no jumping ahead. Trust the order and follow it. Then you will see the results.

Find more information at **www.bethefive.co.uk.**

What then are the five steps that you must follow to ensure success?

DISCUSS

In Discuss we will look at why all good programmes start with a conversation. Knowing who to talk to, when to talk and about what are key aspects to understanding your current environment, staff and customer frustrations, and the benefits that digital could bring to your business. Listening to understand, demystifying business strategies and confusing terminology and acronyms will set you up for a joined-up approach to delivering success led from the top.

DISCOVER

In Discover we will look at your current offerings, what competitors offer and what non-competitors offer. You will learn about taking best practice from a range of industries and applying them to yours. You will look at suppliers and different models, including software ecosystems and cloud-based offerings. You will also Discover the benefits of data that you already hold and how you could use it better. Discover why planning your systems around the data they hold is going to be key to achieving your desired results.

DECIDE

In Decide we will start to bring together the knowledge from Discuss and Discover into an overall strategy that can deliver both quick wins and long-term ambitions. You will have a blueprint for systems and processes that you need to Manage, that can be Improved and those that can be Re-Imagined. You will have the knowledge to understand the business cases behind the strategy and how digital tools will deliver your wider business strategies and corporate goals. You will also have an idea of how to choose the software you are going to buy.

DESIGN

In Design we will learn how to put together the programme plan to ensure that you are delivering the right projects at the right time and ensuring that you are maximising your investment in digital. You will understand where you will get the maximum return across quick wins, and projects that deliver company-wide against those that deliver to individual services. You will be in a position to see where you need additional skills or to outsource projects over those that you can deliver in-house.

DELIVER

In Deliver you will learn that successful delivery depends on repeating the five steps on a smaller, more frequent scale. You will learn how to ensure you receive the right level of information about your projects. You will learn how to deliver your Outcomes and Desired Outcome. You will learn how to measure success and about uptake and adoption of new systems, processes and how to handle culture change.

If you still struggle and need help, then please find my contact details in Chapter 12. We are here to work together. To improve things for everyone. Do not struggle along on your own. There is plenty of support available.

We will now go through each of these steps in more detail.

In the next 5 chapters, we will dive a lot deeper into the 5 Ds. To help you get the absolute most out of this book, I have created a workbook with further advice, insight and space to gather your ideas, notes and answers to the exercises. It is a must have if you are serious about executing this strategy.

Head over to **bethefive.club/workbook** to grab yours before beginning the next 5 chapters.

Discuss

WHAT IS DISCUSS?

Who here makes time for conversations? When was the last time you sat down with a colleague and had a general conversation with them rather than a meeting? When you do have conversations, do you listen to understand or do you listen to reply or debate? In today's busy world business leaders do not put enough time aside to have conversations. This is the key starting point for any digital programme. All too often the conversation stage is bypassed. These often take the form of meetings with multiple guests or presentations where you believe that a conversation has taken

"

Create a
communication
culture.

place. Here, though, I am talking about a real one-to-one conversation, where you are taking the time to speak and more importantly listen to other people's views. Even if you disagree with them, allow yourself to go on a journey to see the other person's points of view and to learn from them.

WHY DISCUSS?

These conversations are important because they will set the tone for the rest of the digital programme. By which I mean that by having meaningful conversations with the right people then any strategy or plan that you come up with is based on actual evidence and feedback. This can then be agreed and approved with those approving fully understanding the implications of what they have agreed. When it then comes to implementing digital, without these open conversations you will hit stumbling blocks as reality dawns or departments that were not part of the conversations refuse to comply. You will also have a greater understanding of your business and, more importantly, of the issues staff face. You will understand the skills within your teams and how that may affect the rollout of projects. Look at *Undercover Boss*, although staged, they do learn a lot about their company. You should not need to be undercover to do this, though. Create a communication culture within your business.

DISCUSS CASE STUDY

During a previous role that I had in local government, the IT department sat within the Resources department, and Resources decided to outsource the service. The winning supplier had based their bid on a reduced service cost by moving the council onto a thin client platform. This essentially moved the council away from laptops and PCs and onto a system based on shared servers. The technical details are not important, but what it did do was transform the way that IT was delivered, to reduce the cost of the IT service. However, although the winning tender was agreed and signed off, not a single signatory understood the implications of a thin client platform and what it meant for their departments. Indeed, because the bidder had not had the right conversations, they had not worked out the cost properly of transitioning the council onto this new platform. Invariably, a six-month project costing about £1m soon turned into a three-year project costing many times more. Although the new contract had been agreed at the top level, it was still down to my team to go and convince each department individually of the benefits to them before we could gain any cooperation from them. This ultimately added months of delays and increased costs to the project. Most of this could have been avoided if the right conversations had happened at the right time. Thin clients were being deployed to reduce IT costs not necessarily to benefit the departments, which was the wrong starting point.

The same is true of the digital strategy I wrote for a council a few years later. The council had an ambitious Customer Experience programme and I had to deliver a strategy to enable the outcomes to be delivered. It was clear that legacy technology was going to inhibit the amount of change that services could make. The strategy was therefore relatively straightforward in that we needed to replace the legacy systems and join up services using a platform and ecosystem of applications. All straightforward, but at the time it was also quite revolutionary in the sector.

However, it was a five-year strategy for a reason, that mainly being it would take five years to fully implement and embed it. There would obviously be wins and efficiencies throughout the five years, but the totality of the strategy was large and would take time. After many senior meetings on the programme, including a non-technical manager attending a US conference with me to report back that the software was fit for purpose, the strategy was approved by the Corporate Management Team and then closely followed by Cabinet approval.

This is when the alarm bells started ringing. At the time I was pretty pleased with how easily the strategy was being approved. I had expected some kickback on some of the elements of the strategy, but none were forthcoming. Not that they were controversial, but they were very different to the norm and quite left field in a rather static and legacy-based industry. It soon became very clear that most of the approvers did not fully understand the strategy and the implications of it despite numerous con-versations. Some of the approvers, dare I say it, clearly had not read it. None of the approvers had had any mean-ingful conversations with any of their reports about what was being approved.

On the first day of implementing the strategy, the business analysts were taken off the project and re-as-signed by a senior project sponsor. From that point on it went downhill quickly as they were crucial to its success.

Without going too deep into any failures, the issue here was quite simple. The conversations were generally one-way. It was me explaining the strategy to colleagues, who seemed to listen intently, but they did not under-stand it and did not say that they did not understand it. Whether this was through not wanting to look bad, not wanting to understand or a lack of interest, it ultimately led to failure. The conversations you have must be honest and open. The managers were expected to feed this information down to their teams, but how could they do that if they had not understood it in the first place?

The role digital is going to play in businesses in the future is too important to keep quiet if you do not under-stand some of the basics. If you are not able to have a proper conversation with your IT team, your staff, and your customers, then you will not implement digital tools properly and efficiently. You cannot afford to ignore it or brush it off as someone else's job.

STEPS FOR DISCUSS

Once you have considered the fact that you do not have enough conversations and do not set enough time aside, then you'll need to be considering what the conversations are that you should be having and with whom.

1. Discuss with your staff

First and foremost, you should be speaking to your staff. You should be finding out what elements of their role they struggle with and where the constraints are in allowing them to be more efficient. What you are aiming to achieve is to have enough information at your hands to sign off and approve a digital strategy that we will come onto in Decide. You need to know what challenges the strategy is going to help you overcome and the only way to do that is to start internally.

Does your sales team lack some basic data on customers that would help them sell? Does Finance have too much of a reliance on spreadsheets still and rekeying information across multiple sheets? Does HR have a complete record of all your staff and their skillset that could help at peak times? Which processes take up too much time or are too inefficient? These are all things that we will be looking at improving with digital.

There will always be gripes and issues that staff have with the systems that they use. There will also be positive aspects that they do like. It may not actually be systems that you use. Maybe they have tools that they use in their personal and social lives that they like and use a lot. Or maybe they prefer Facebook to Instagram. Find out why and what challenges they have between one or the other. You are trying to build a complete picture here to enable you to really drive forwards as a business.

Which companies do your staff buy from, and how do they enjoy the experience? Even home shopping, Asda, Tesco, Ocado, plus all the others. What do they find simple, and what elements are annoying? You do not need to chat to every single person. You need to get a real feel for how your staff view the digital world. This will also give you a good indication of how much work you are going to have to do when potentially you move staff onto new systems or new ways of working.

2. Discuss with IT

You also need to speak to IT, whether this is an in-house team or you use a third party. Explain your aims and ask for their view on the current estate. What is hampering your ambition, and what changes do they think you would need to make? You will probably find out a lot about your current estate that you were not aware of. IT are a part of the solution, but they should not be leading on digital. Ensure that they take the time to explain the systems to you rather than using acronyms or technical terminology. Do not be afraid to say that you do not understand. They are the guardians of your current systems and will know more about your set up than anyone else. Use this as an opportunity to learn from them. At the same time, let them learn from you. Bring your relationship closer.

3. Discuss with your customers

As well as staff, the next most important group to speak to are your customers. Hopefully, you already receive feedback from your customers on the products or services that you provide. Do you also ask them about each step of the process they went through to buy from you or to contact you in customer services? Most customer service surveys ask if you were satisfied with the answer or product. Not if they found it easy to find help, would have liked an online service, whether they prefer to phone, or how they felt buying from you. If you are going to work out how to delight your customers, then you need to be asking the right questions about their experience.

Potentially, you could do this through a survey that you send out to them but having a phone call or a face to face conversation will give you much more of an insight. People like conversations and like being asked their opinion on something. Your job is to facilitate these conversations and then listen to the feedback you are given.

The size of your company is also irrelevant at this point. The local barber that I use has six staff. They now have a system where you book your hair appointment online, you can search for a time and which barber you wish to cut your hair. Once booked, you receive a text message confirming the booking and then a reminder of the booking nearer the time and on the day. It takes me seconds to flick through their diary and find an appointment that suits me.

The barbers themselves then have all their bookings on their computer in the shop and know exactly who is due when and for what cut. It's far away from the days of having to phone up and have a receptionist flick through a massive diary on the desk, trying to find a slot for your favourite hairdresser and writing you in. Then they would give you a card with your appointment time and date on the back, which you invariably lost. Then you had to phone back to get the receptionist to flick through the diary to find your booking. It is all about the efficiency of the service you provide. No more difficulty in booking appointments or turning up with no appointment and sitting and waiting to be served.

It may not be for everyone, some may still like to phone, but booking online is the more prevalent method and will only grow. My barbers still have some steps to take. They still need to be able to take payments online too, but I am sure that will come. I am always asked about the booking process during the cut too. They are constantly asking for feedback, so please get out there and speak to your customers. They are a huge asset for you. Ask them about the service you provide, not just the end product they receive. Even if you do this in groups or one to one, it does not matter. During this stage you need to be all about information gathering and ensuring that there is a feedback loop in place to gather the information that will help your business.

4. Discuss with friends and family

First colleagues and customers and now we move on to friends and family. Yes, that is right, I am going to make you speak to your family. Like your colleagues and customers, they will all use digital tools in everyday life. Find out which ones they like and why. Speak to the older generations of your family, but also the younger ones. You will get such a varied mix of answers. My son is currently obsessed with Fortnite and TikTok. Last year it was Minecraft and YouTube. Next year it will be something different; but even at 10 he shows me things that amaze me. An ex-colleague of mine recently posted on Facebook that his 20-month-old daughter has worked out how to screencast from the iPad to the television. That is incredible, but it just shows how much effort has gone into making the iPad very simplistic and intuitive to use. The next generation are growing up with these tools as normal everyday items. Include their views in your research. Similarly, the older generation will have their views. Some will like technology and be using it, some will not. Find out why and figure the differences. Think about how you can use this information in your business. Are you offering an experience that a toddler could use?

Your friends… speak to them too. What do their businesses use? What do they like about your site, competitor sites and services? Although I am quite anti the armchair digital experts, who will tell you what software to use without understanding your need, asking friends for their experience and knowledge is fine. Just do not blindly go and buy the same tools they use just because they like them, or their mate told them to buy it and he is really into computers. We are just information gathering here and broadening your knowledge.

As you can see from this stage, it is all about gathering a background of information that you will find beneficial as we go into the next stage of Discover and then onto Decide. It will also help you with both Design and Deliver as you will have a much better understanding of the skillset of your colleagues.

5. Discuss with your current providers

Finally, there is one last group of people that you need to have conversations with. This one crosses over slightly into Discover but it is important to do this early on before you move too far into the next step. You may not want to speak to them, but please speak to either the reps for the software that you already have or experts in the industry that know your current tools. At this point we are not looking at buying anything. You do need to know whether any of the tools you already own and use have additional functionality that you were unaware of that might be of use to you. Obviously, take anything that the reps say with a pinch of salt, I am yet to meet one whose system does not do everything or could do everything with a bit of development. Try and get them to stick to the facts of what it does today and any best practice information and advice they have. You might be able to avoid a project altogether.

EXERCISE

To make doing these exercises easier, I have created a workbook for you that will give further depth, advice and examples. Having this resource alongside the book will be vital to your success. If you haven't already, you need to go and grab it at **bethefive.club/workbook**

1. List 10 people that you can have a conversation with.

2. List three companies you enjoy buying from.

3. List three reasons why you enjoy buying from them.

4. List three companies you dislike buying from.

5. List three reasons why you dislike buying from them.

6. Ask the same question of your list of 10 people.

7. Are there any similarities?

8. What does this tell you about your experiences of buying from companies?

9. Ask the same questions of your business.

From these exercises you will understand the different views people have towards using digital.

This only looks at buying from companies, but this can be extended into all types of interactions and your own internal processes. You will be gathering a range of views that may not be the same as yours. It is about expanding your knowledge. You will now have the background information required to move to the next stage.

SUMMARY

You should now have an absolute plethora of information available to you. You will need to have kept track of that information, and made notes of people's opinions, views, and advice. You will have a good understanding of issues across the business. What staff find simple or hard, what customers like or dislike with your business and what friends and family like. Some of it you may not want to hear but you need the feedback, both good and bad, to enable you to take the business forward. Allow plenty of time for this stage and revisit it as often as you can. Understanding this from the outset will really help you to become efficient. We are now going to use that information as the basis for the next stage.

Discover

WHAT IS DISCOVER?

You have now had as many conversations as you can. You have a good understanding of the issues and opportunities that staff and customers have fed back to you. You have Discussed with your IT department about current technology and now it is time to start looking at opportunities further afield. Discover is your opportunity to do some real-world research into solutions that you have unearthed during Discuss.

WHY DISCOVER?

The Discover stage is important as you are now build-

ing your knowledge of digital. You have that core understanding from Discuss and you are going to need to turn
that into a digital strategy in Decide. This step lets you
Discover what some of those solutions might look like. It
is about improving your knowledge based on your own
findings, which will help you to approve the best possible strategy for your business. You want the best outcomes for your business, so you will need to know what
is available. Your IT team will help but you are the leader
that is going to hold this together. You are going to solve
problems you have Discussed with technology that you
have Discovered. If you do not understand what the art
of the possible could be then how will you know if the
strategy being delivered is right for you? This element
is a time-consuming exercise and is also one that you
will need to return to time and time again as technology
and business models advance. It is going to be a lifelong
journey for you.

DISCOVER CASE STUDY

One key element of Discover is looking at the systems
that you already use. I made the decision to move a
council from Microsoft Office to Google's G Suite. There
were many underlying reasons for this, which I will not go
into here. However, what I Discovered was how attached
to Microsoft Excel some people were. There are many
people professing to be experts but, in reality, they can do
only a handful of quite basic tasks. Excel itself is incredi-

"

You want the best outcomes for your business, so you will need to know what is available.

bly powerful, can handle incredible amounts of data and multiple complex equations and sums. Yet there you are thinking you are an expert because you can do a pivot table. But try taking Excel off someone and giving them a more basic, and possibly free, version and they will give you every excuse as to why they need to keep Excel. When you break down the tasks that were actually being completed on Excel then there was no reason why 95% of the estate could not easily move to Google Sheets. Even I decided not to take on finance over that one.

It was a battle, though. It really was. You would have thought I was taking a child off some of them. If I had put my arm across the top of their monitor, they would not have even known if it was Sheets or Excel. Adding columns and adding some colours to them is advanced. So, having Discovered that most people did not even use 5% of the power of Excel, I also Discovered that they did not want to give it up for anything.

Here is where we hit familiarity of systems rather than having the right system for the right job. They like Excel because they are comfortable with it. They know where the buttons are to do the tasks they do, but are you paying a premium for a Ferrari when you only need a Vauxhall? If you don't believe me, then grab a copy of the Dummies guide to Excel and open it towards the back and start looking at the more complex tasks you can complete with it and then tell me who's an expert! There is an annual Excel competition that takes place with entrants from across the globe. These are the real experts!

I had done my Discovery on Excel and its use in the business. I had Discovered alternatives that included an upgrade to O365, a number of free options as well as G Suite. I had Decided that the best option for the council to Deliver its long-term aims would be G Suite. It tied into our ecosystem better than anything else.

This example is straightforward as Excel is a tool virtually all of us will have used at some point. We've all probably only really dabbled with 2-5% of its actual capabilities, though, but you need to apply some of this thinking across the other systems you use. This is why we do Discuss first, as you need to understand where your colleagues are at with their knowledge and how easy or hard making a move will be.

STEPS FOR DISCOVER

1. Discover what you currently offer

A simple exercise to start with here is to look at what software you already use. It always amazes me that leaders often do not know the size of their estate, the tools that are in use across it and for what reason they are used. Larger companies will often find that they have multiple systems designed to do the exact same task used by different departments. By stating that their software does one or two things differently to other comparative software, they have convinced procurement to buy them a shinier version of an old product already in use. What you will also Discover is that there is software, often expensive, that is only used for a small element of what it can do as it is not being used efficiently.

As mentioned in Discuss, you may need to bring reps or consultants in to review some of your systems. The most efficient thing you can do is to make the most of the tools you already have, and this could possibly mean that you can remove other tools from your estate. Even with Excel, there are cheaper and even free alternatives, but do not just use price as the limiting factor. It is about your staff and how well they can do their jobs with the tools you give them.

You may also Discover tools being used by staff that are not corporately approved tools. Shadow IT, as it is known, can be frowned upon in a lot of companies, but it provides you with some very useful information. It shows you where your staff are struggling with the tools you have provided and what they are doing with their shadow tools. Use this as an opportunity to learn, not to block tools.

Shadow IT is the use of digital tools that have not been provided by your IT team. Often, you will find staff that have apps on their phones that they use for note taking or for completing tasks, but this can take many forms. A lot of businesses try to ban this completely and lock down systems so that staff cannot use them. I have seen businesses issue iPhones to staff and then remove all the features and benefits of giving them an iPhone. It makes no sense to do this.

The only reason staff are using shadow IT is because

they struggle with the tools you have given them or have found a more efficient way of doing things. You should be embracing this knowledge and sharing it. Ensure that IT can then evaluate the tools and, as long as there are no glaring security issues, allow them to be used. This is not a case of the 'computer says no', this is the computer says yes, unless there is a real issue. It is much easier to ban a tool than it is to do the necessary homework to Discover how it is used and for what purposes.

Discover which systems you already have, how they are used, and the skills that you need to develop to support them.

2. Discover what data you have and need

The next thing to Discover is data. Data is going to be the lifeblood of your company going forwards. It is more important than the software in many ways. To give you an easy analogy, we will start thinking about wine. Maybe now is the right time to pour yourself a glass. Chances are you have chosen a nice wine glass to pour your wine into. If you did not have a wine glass, then maybe you have used a cup or a mug or – if you are really desperate – a jam jar. The truth is the vessel that the wine sits in is less important than the wine itself. The vessel can have an effect, it may make the wine seem nicer, it may give it more air, but ultimately the real taste comes down to the wine itself.

When you start to Discover your data, keep this analogy in mind. You will see lots of flashy software with all sorts of bells and whistles added. What is important, though, is what data does it collect or hold and what does it then allow you to do with that data. What information is it giving you? Does it help you keep the data clean, or is it going to cork your wine? Start with the data and what you need to achieve with it and from there you can start to Discover what software is available.

The second data perspective to think about is then what data you already hold, why you hold it and what you can do with it using your current systems. What could you do better? Can you re-use the data? Can you keep it in use? Or is it lost after being processed? Is there any data that you are missing that could enrich your current data? How do you think you could collect extra data? Go back to some of the discussions you have had with staff and customers. Could any of their frustrations be fixed by having better data? Knowing your customers in detail is going to allow you to serve them better and with a more personalised service than you currently can.

I recently undertook a small survey with business owners on Social Listening. It was a simple survey of who uses it, with a straight 'yes', 'no', and 'never heard of it' as the answers. Despite being around for several years, the results were that approximately 65% had never heard of it, 30% had heard of it but did not use it and only 5% were using it. If you've heard of it and decided it adds no value to your business to collect that data then that's fine, but for 65% of business owners to not even be aware that it is a thing is appalling. It suggests a lack of understanding of digital and a lack of conversations with people who do. It even shows a lack of having someone that you can rely on to proactively come to you with suggestions for how it could help. And, before you ask, if you are in the 65% then no, I am not going to tell you what it is either. Go and Discover it for yourselves and the data it can give you!

3. Discover the wider market

We have looked at what software you already have and how you are using it. We have looked at what data you hold and how you could use it better. Now we are going to look a bit wider and Discover what is happening both in your sector and in other sectors. You do not necessarily need to copy anyone, but you do need to be aware of what is happening outside of your business. Two companies that failed to do this properly were Blockbuster and Kodak. Both companies had failed to see the speed at which their industry had started moving in a different direction and were then too slow to react when other companies were rapidly growing into their sectors.

Although most leaders will be looking at other companies on a regular basis, how often is this done from a digital perspective? Looking at how they are serving their customers or becoming more efficient in what they do? Most of us use digital tools in our lives on an everyday basis. How often do you stop to think about the ones you use? What benefits do they give you as a customer? What benefits do you think the company that provides them gets? What frustrates you about them? What do you genuinely like? Do you have a list of these? If not, you can start now and create one. Keep it somewhere safe until we get to the next stage. Each time you use a service, make a note of what you like or did not like, how you felt as a customer and how valued you were. Are you likely to go back to use the same service again? Or did it frustrate you? Did it take too long to buy something? Did you receive a follow-up to your complaint or comment? Keep track of these and compare the experience to how your customers feel. What did you Discover from them during the Discuss stage? Consider your industry sector but also those of other sectors that you use.

You will be using this information in the next stage, so do as much research as possible into the market. Should a competitor come along and completely change the industry then you are going to need to be flexible enough in systems and processes to adapt to meet the challenge. Maybe, through looking at how you can deliver services more efficiently, you will be the next Netflix, even if on a smaller scale, that does transform your industry. Constantly be thinking and challenging yourself on how this could help you deliver your services more efficiently.

4. Discover the software you need

From here we can start looking at software and software providers. It is useful to spend time really doing some research here. I see lots of companies that have systems that have been recommended to them by a friend as it works for their business, even if their business is completely different. With over 1,500 different solutions just for marketing out there, going on the system your friend uses might be completely the wrong solution for you. Similarly, with CRMs, there are hundreds out there. As I mentioned above, look at these systems from the perspective of what value they will add to the data that you hold or collect. Do not be impressed by how shiny and flashy they have made it look. Underneath that flashy exterior is just a collection of tables that hold data and place it in the right position on the screen. Look at the system that treats your data best, not the one that looks the whizziest.

As part of this it is also crucial to look at product ecosystems. I am a big fan of Salesforce.com. They have some incredible products available that work well and can allow you to perform all sorts of tasks. What impresses me most, though, is the ecosystem of compatible tools that are designed to work with Salesforce. Salesforce have their own online app store called the AppExchange where you can find a tool for practically anything that you can think of. The majority are from third party companies, but they are all designed to work seamlessly with the Salesforce products. This offers you a huge benefit by not requiring the complex process of trying to get two systems from two providers to pass data between each other.

Although it may not be the solution for you, you do ultimately pay a price for this ecosystem. When looking at software think about the whole ecosystem of complementary products available. It is a useful piece of research to do, by looking at the product set one company offers, which includes a CRM for both Service and Sales, a Marketing product suite, and a Business Intelligence product. They have inbuilt Artificial Intelligence plus they give developers the tools to build products on their platform. It really is the best ecosystem that you will come across and the partnerships they have are second to none. Use them as the benchmark for any alternative solutions that you look at.

In a similar vein, Microsoft used to be a solution that was focused very much on themselves. It was Microsoft or a competitor. Since Satya Nadella took over as CEO there has been a concerted shift to Microsoft and a competitor. Making sure their systems can be part of a wider ecosystem and not just Microsoft or bust. You need to be asking yourself whether you just want a standalone system or whether you want one where sales are linked to service and service to finance and finance to business intelligence.

Or would you like to have to download information and upload to the next system? Or have someone build you a process that moves data overnight, so that you are always a day behind? No, you do not.

As I mentioned in the previous section, ecosystems are something you need to be thinking about. By having a software ecosystem, you can look to change your business to also have a staff ecosystem and focus on product teams not service teams. We will cover this aspect later in the book.

EXERCISE

The following exercises, advice, examples and space to answer them are all in your workbook. If you haven't got it, grab it at: **bethefive.club/workbook**

1. List the market leaders in your industry.

2. What online presence do they have?

3. List your favourite brands that have an online presence.

4. How do these differ from your industry?

5. Research Cloud computing. Look at Software-as-a-Service, Infrastructure-as-a-Service and Platform-as-a-Service.

6. Research the Salesforce AppExchange. How big an ecosystem do they have? How does this compare to your current providers?

7. Research companies such as:

   ❍ Amazon Web Services

   ❍ Google Cloud Platform and G Suite

   ❍ Microsoft Azure

   ❍ Salesforce

   ❍ Box

   ❍ Sprinklr

- BounceX (Wunderkind)

- Tableau

- ThoughtSpot

- Okta

- Celonis

This will increase your knowledge of the types of providers and the wide range of services available. Find more examples in each of these categories.

Research Artificial Intelligence, Machine Learning, and Internet of Things (IoT). What are they and how could they help your business?

After completing these exercises, you will under-stand how businesses are using digital and have started your research into what software options there are out there for you. There are thousands of options, but by overlaying the information you uncovered in Discuss you will be able to narrow the list down to tools that help solve the issues you know about and are relevant to your business.

SUMMARY

During this step you should have been able to match a lot of what you found in Discuss to what you have found in Discover. You should have Discovered a lot of options available to you. New technologies, new ideas you had never heard of, and new models of IT. There is absolutely no shame in sitting on Google and looking at companies and suppliers and seeing what they offer. You may need to clarify points from Discuss as you have now looked at solutions and the wider market. Now in your notes you can overlay the Discover information against the Discuss information and start to formulate a plan of where you need to be heading as a business and therefore what your digital strategy needs to be. These two stages were key to aligning your digital strategy with your business strategy. It may have even changed some of your views on your business strategy too. It is about opening yourself up to the world of digital and embracing it as something to benefit from, not to fear.

Never stop Discovering.

Decide

WHAT IS DECIDE?

In the previous stage, I told you to pour yourself a glass of wine. It is now time to put that down and put the kettle on and make a tea or coffee and get yourself comfortable. As I mentioned at the start of this section of the book, Decide is really going to be the key stage that you as a business leader need to be on top of. You are going to have to concentrate now. Decide is going to focus on your digital strategy and how you achieve one that works for your business. We will be taking the Discuss and Discover stages and bringing them together into a plan that will enable you to achieve your business goals.

"

An important
part of any
digital strategy
is being able to
measure success.

WHY DECIDE?

How is your digital strategy going to help the business achieve or accelerate its plans? A strategy is, 'a plan of action designed to achieve a long-term or overall aim'. Therefore, this is your most basic starting point. That it is a plan of action. What you are going to do.

However, key to the strategy is the part about achieving a long-term or overall aim. This is where so many digital strategies go wrong and the reason that the failure rates are so high. The aim of digital is to make your business more efficient at what it does. Most strategies I read focus on making the IT department more efficient. They have very generic phrasing and terminology in them and a lack of clarity over the aims. They have not factored in that they are a service department to the business.

Decide will help you ensure that your digital strategy will focus on achieving the business aims and outcomes. It will set out your aims for the next 3-5 years. It will give you measurable outcomes that you can work towards and achieve success.

DECIDE CASE STUDY

An important part of any digital strategy is being able to measure success. One of the reasons so many digital projects fail to deliver business value is because they were implemented without the understanding of what the desired outcomes were. To differentiate between outcomes and desired outcomes, I will use an example of buying and installing a piece of software to run marketing campaigns. The outcome of this project was to implement the software. This meant the business can run marketing campaigns, gaining insights into the material sent out – who had opened emails, who had forwarded, engagement and response rates – and it could all be directly integrated into the Salesforce CRM.

However, the desired outcome of buying the software was that the company sold more. Therefore, it was about providing better-qualified leads to the Sales Team. If the software was not producing these leads, which Sales could turn into a customer, then there was no point having the software. It is this key differentiator that often makes or breaks a project.

Marketing software companies know this and therefore, on top of providing the software, you will often also receive a whole host of information on writing eye-catching emails and the best time to send them. They will suggest how to follow up with leads and a host of other relevant information in a variety of mediums, from face to face, webinars, blogs, and reference pages on their websites. They know that they need to ensure that the customer hits the desired outcome of more sales for the software to be deemed a success. Hitting just the outcome is not enough.

It is important to note here that different roles within a business have different desired outcomes from the same project. Being able to list these at the start of the project ensured that I could measure proper success and ensure that the delivery team were working to an agreed set of outcomes. Marketing, Sales, Operations and Finance all had different desired outcomes. It is no wonder so many projects fail to deliver business benefits if the research into what the true benefits are have not been completed first.

A simple exercise that I asked colleagues to undertake to establish these outcomes and desired outcomes was to complete the sentence:

'I want....... because....... because......'

I use this method as the second 'because' makes you change your language slightly to fit the sentence structure and it is sometimes quite hard to word. In other words, it makes people think.

In this instance, the desired outcomes were all similar but slightly different. I had to look at Marketing needing to run better campaigns to give Sales better quality leads, to convert them more quickly, to ensure that the Finance hits the forecast revenue figures. All pulling in the same direction but with a slightly different requirement and measure of success. Understanding the subtleties upfront will allow for the measured success of the software implementation and usage. Because I had completed the upfront work and ensured I could measure success from the strategy based on business outcomes, the project went much more smoothly than it would have done without knowing this information.

Understanding the outcomes and business goals at this early stage of your digital programme will enable you to undertake this evaluation. Do not try to find out what the outcomes are once you have started a project. If you know what business outcomes you want to achieve first, then you can align your digital strategy to them.

STEPS FOR DECIDE

1. Decide your strategy

I want to see specifics in your strategy. How is the IT dept, whether in house, outsourced or a partner, going to help you to become more efficient as a business? How will they help finance? How will they help sales to sell more? How will they help marketing to get more leads?

The starting point for a digital strategy is to find the other strategies and plans that relate to the business, be it around growth, lower costs, higher margins, better customer service, service change or customer retention. The list can be endless, depending on the sector. But all businesses should have a business strategy or plan. Councils will have corporate and service plans. Government departments will often have key priorities. It does not matter which sector you are in. You have to know what you want digital to help you to achieve before you can implement it.

This is your starting point. When you look at it from this perspective then the digital strategy becomes much easier to write and much more relevant to your business.

I have seen many digital strategies that do not have

any references to the wider business. Ones that do not have a plan. Ones that are being written despite the business not having a plan. How can you possibly write a strategy for a service department when you do not know what the plan for the business is?

I have seen some appalling strategies that forget who the customer is. I have had to review Shared Services in the Public Sector that had written strategies about how they were going to make themselves super-efficient. They would deliver a set number of projects to the council because they, as the provider, wanted to become more efficient. They completely missed the point. They were supposed to be making the council more efficient. It is a common mistake that I see all too often. Do not make the same mistake.

You have gone through Discuss and Discover first to understand your users and their requirements. You, as a leader, will also know your business ambitions and your departmental outcomes.

2. Decide on your leadership role

It would seem like a lot of the problems stem from quite poor strategies or a lack of outcomes to deliver to. Who then approves the strategies? Most of the time it is the CEO or similarly senior management. Often, they are accused of doing this in isolation from the business. Hence why you are going through this methodical approach. It is very important to be absolutely clear here for one moment. **You should not be writing the digital strategy.** The previous stages are not about you being able to write a strategy. They are about you receiving a digital strategy that you can understand, review, and challenge. It should relate to your knowledge of the business and the market and then be approved based on an understanding of how it is going to make your business more efficient. Too many leaders still receive a nice document, maybe 30 pages of writing, maybe a nice PowerPoint to go along with it, and they skim read it. They see a few buzzwords, they might throw in a question ('What about Blockchain?'), and then they approve it.

They have not understood a word of it and certainly not any of the implications, nor the business benefits. And off IT go to try and implement their generic strategy and we end up with a 95% failure rate. Your IT department should be fully aware of what you expect from the strategy. In fact, they should be completing the same five steps as you.

Key to understanding your digital strategy and having it deliver clear business efficiencies is to have taken yourself through the Discuss and Discover stages first. These are the key groundwork and foundation stages for you to improve your digital knowledge. To understand your staff and customer frustrations. To have Discussed difficulties with your IT department. To have Discovered how you can use data better. To have Discovered different delivery models for software. To have Discovered ecosystems. To now be in a place to really challenge and dissect your new strategy.

This is your moment to shine. To stand up and ensure you are getting this right. You do not need to understand everything about digital. You do not need to know how to code. You do not need to know how an API works. You do need to know how all these things can help you. You need to be able to have a conversation with IT about the strategy. How is it delivering against customer frustrations? How will your staff be more efficient? You can no longer just pay lip service to this. Getting your strategy right will enable you to be able to sell it to the business. You will be able to explain why the changes are taking place and what this means to their jobs. Imagine how eager salespeople will be to adopt new software if you tell them it will help them close more deals and earn more commission. They will be chomping at the bit. Tell them you are replacing a piece of software as IT has a strategy and need to change and you will find reluctance and a lack of buy-in. To be honest, they will probably just start using a spreadsheet or something else. Make sure the digital work is led by its need to achieve service aims.

Technology projects turn people off unless they can see what is in it for them. Lack of uptake of new tools and new ways of working is the second most significant reason for projects failing. This stems from not having a clear strategy that shows the business benefits. Many staff just feel like IT is doing another project and changing things and therefore do not give any buy-in or give any time. A solid strategy with real leadership stood behind it will help alleviate these problems. Having already gone through the Discuss stage with your staff, they will know that they have been listened to and are part of the solution.

This is not IT seeing some shiny toys that they want to play with and implement. This is a real desire to make your business more efficient. From implementing this strategy, you will find a digital company culture is much easier to instil. As the popular phrase does not go, 'strategy will eat culture for breakfast'. A good digital strategy will help you build a good digital culture, with everyone on the same page and pulling in the same direction. A good culture will not necessarily lead to a good strategy. Growing that digital culture, or digital mindset, will not only help your business, but it will help develop your staff. And you need to lead it.

3. Decide on IT's role

All too often you will see digital teams trying to set the world to rights and fixing all the world's problems. Using their own language and not involving those from outside IT. They are adopting a technology first approach. They are working with good intentions, but they have not done the necessary background work to understand what needs to be delivered. They do not understand that people who do not understand digital are involved and are their customers. They have started running before they can walk. They need to rewind and come back to the company. As much as the leaders need to go through Discuss, IT also must do this. We joke when we watch programmes like

The IT Crowd, teams resigned to the basement, who ask you to turn it off and on again. But these are the same guys that will help you deliver the most value for your company if you use them correctly.

If only IT and the business could speak the same language. Here is your next task with the strategy. Remove the jargon. No-one outside of IT knows (or cares) what it means. We can all use industry specific acronyms and terminology. Telling someone in finance that you are going to build some APIs and move to infrastructure as a service is meaningless. Tell them that you are going to connect two systems to stop them having to manually rekey data and move the systems to a third-party provider to ensure stability and less downtime. These are the messages that staff need to hear and will actively play a part in delivering. If they see a strategy document as a set of indecipherable words and phrases that mean nothing to them, they are likely to not read, or skim read at best. This is what had happened to me before. I had a lip service strategy that was not fully understood. It therefore hit problems as soon as delivery started and that was with the majority of the terminology removed. Getting people to read a strategy is hard enough. Then getting messages passed down from senior managers to middle managers about how and why the strategy was going to make their jobs easier and more efficient is even harder. Make sure whoever in IT is ultimately responsible for the strategy can write in clear language that everyone can understand. If they can do this, then you will know that you have the right people leading the department. IT must be able to explain the business benefits in the strategy, and these must be based on actual real issues and benefits that have previously been Discussed and Discovered. No-one outside of IT wants to read a digital strategy. You must sell it to the reader. What is in it for them?

4. Decide on your current tools

Unless you are a brand-new company, then it is highly likely that you already have technology that you use. Whilst we focus on moving your company forwards to be an efficiency machine, we must consider your current estate. You cannot just remove or change everything you currently have. Instead, you can categorise your current offerings with those that you want to move to in the future. Here IT will play another fundamental role. As you look at your new strategy and any prerequisites you may have, you can break your estate down into three categories. These are Manage, Improve and Re-Imagine. Not only does this help you visualise the estate and give you a start of a plan to move forwards, it also helps you define what skills you will need in IT. This will also force IT to speak to the business about their processes.

Quite simply, in three boxes you can label software and technology in one of the three categories.

Manage is software that you currently have that you cannot or do not want to replace. It may be legacy software, but it will need someone to look after it and keep it working.

Improve is software that you may want to replace. It may be old, even if it is cloud, or not benefiting you as a business. You need to think about how you will move to a new product or add products on top of existing software (a digital form that captures information and feeds directly into you CRM might be an improvement).

Re-Imagine is then looking at those processes where you do not currently have a piece of software. You can look at this from a totally blank piece of paper and think about buying or building something completely new. The airline apps for boarding cards is a good example of this.

Depending on your size, you may have multiple copies of this template relating to your departments and one overarching company-wide one. If you are relatively small you may only need to do this once. If each template is linked to the business outcomes, then formulating a plan for both resources and software to replace starts to become quite simple. Although this is an IT task it should be undertaken in consultation with the services it covers – Discuss, Discover, and Decide.

5. Decide on your strategy timespan

Another key component of the strategy is how long you are going to be planning on having one in place. I usually recommend a digital strategy with a lifespan of 3-5 years. That seems like a long time, but it is necessary given how long most projects take to implement and embed. There is also an element of people and process change within each of these projects. By having a longer-term strategy, you can undertake projects in a sensible timeframe. This gives staff and customers time to use and feed-back on their experiences before you move onto the next project. The longer length of the strategy also allows all staff to buy into the end result that you are working to. This is a key message to be given. You will find that you have some quick wins along the journey but there must be an end state that you want to achieve with your strategy. There will be steps that you need to take to get there. In some cases, you may have to take a step backwards before you can take two steps forwards. There may be times where you must rekey some information twice, whilst you change systems or build the connections. Clarity over the end goal will help staff understand why this is nec-essary. This will come down to how easy you have made the strategy to read and understand for staff that do not necessarily understand digital terminology.

However, and it is a big however, just because you have written a five-year strategy, it does not mean you are now fixed to stick to it rigidly for that period. Depending on your industry, you should be reviewing the strategy every 6-12 months. The speed at which technology and industries can change, or are changing, means that you now must be on top of this and always reviewing. Go back to Discuss and Discover at regular intervals. Do not be like Kodak and Blockbuster that had strategies and models that they stuck to rigidly and then could not implement a new one quickly enough. You need to be much more agile than this. You need to be able to respond to changes in market demand or services.

As your business needs change and develop, your digital strategy will need to be able to move with this. New technologies are always coming to market. Hopefully through the Discover stage you have started to get to grips with some of the terminology linked to these and can see how your business could benefit from them. It is non-stop, though, and there are constantly new trends emerging. Companies like Amazon Web Services are able to release hundreds of new products and services every year. Again, you do not need to understand how they all work, but you do need to understand what is out there and how it can help you.

You will constantly be learning, but it will be for the benefit of yourself and your business. You cannot always rely on IT to keep an eye on all trends and then to be able to explain how they can help your business departments. As a leader you do need to be able to do this, as should all your senior managers. Senior staff that do not understand digital will not be useful to your business in the long term. You are becoming a technology company with your specific service on top, so you need to start thinking like one.

6. Decide on governance

Once you have Decided on your 3-5-year digital strategy there is now one more big decision to be made. How are you going to Decide which digital tools you are going to buy?

That is a big leap from Deciding a strategy to buying software. Surely there are some steps in between? Yes, that is true to a point. I have written a strategy previously and included all the tools that were going to be purchased in the strategy too. It had been designed that way from day one, and I knew what the tools were that were going to deliver success as I knew the challenges that were being faced. For you, this may not be so easy, but do not worry. You do not need to know the exact tools and who provides them. At this stage you should be working out how you are going to Decide what is bought.

Your strategy will naturally be leading you down a certain route towards the types of tools you will need. For the specific details of which ones you buy, are you going to have a purchasing board? Are you going to trust IT's recommendations? Are you going to have a process to show how the tools meet the strategy? Who has the final sign off and do they understand the end goal? Is there going to be a digital policy or checklist of requirements? Is it part of a wider ecosystem?

At this stage, it is perfectly reasonable to have a cloud first policy (not strategy). This means you can assess digital tools against a checklist. If there is no solution that is as-a-service, then maybe hosted is your second option. A data centre your third option and, finally, on premise as a last resort, as an example. This will be something you need to agree on internally. Make sure you have a digital procurement board or sign-off of some sort that shows how a certain type of tool meets your aims and have it approved at a senior level before you purchase anything. Oversight of digital procurement and having a set of principles to follow will help you smooth the journey. Agree this upfront and it will help with later decision making.

7. Decide on how to measure success

So how do you know how a digital tool will meet your needs when purchasing one? The first thing to do is Decide what those needs are and what you expect from the system.

What this then helps with is creating a template for a very simple business case. It does not need to be overly onerous, but it should be able to state that you are going to be buying a certain digital tool, because it meets the needs of the strategy. In purchasing and implementing the software, you understand that it will need to deliver the agreed outcomes and desired outcomes. You may well have a simple Return on Investment calculation in there too. That is really all you need to sign off the purchase. Everyone should then be very clear in why you are doing the project, what tools you are implementing and what outcomes you are delivering. When projects then get to your digital procurement board, you have now made the task of approving purchases much simpler.

EXERCISE

The following exercises, advice, examples and space to answer them are all in your workbook. If you haven't got it, grab it at: **bethefive.club/workbook**

1. Find your business or departmental strategies or plans.

2. How could the applications you looked at in Discover help you to achieve these aims?

3. If you have a current IT or digital strategy, does it show how digital will help you to meet your aims as a business? What are the gaps?

4. Find digital strategies online. Local government often publish these, if you cannot find business ones. Do these strategies show how they will help the business? Are their outcomes featured in the strategy?

5. Work out what you would change in them to deliver outcomes.

6. List 10 things that you would hypothetically challenge the CEO on regarding their strategy.

Completing these exercises will improve your knowledge around what a good digital strategy should look like. It should have clear outcomes related to business benefits. Overlay Discuss and Discover to your strategies and see if they are delivering your requirements.

SUMMARY

From this stage we should now have been able to read your digital strategy and match plans with business requirements. You should be able to easily see these. If you cannot then the strategy will need to be rewritten. Hopefully, you can now see the importance of the Discuss and Discover stages in ensuring that the document that has been produced will deliver these benefits. You will be able to look at the strategy and look at some of the outcomes that your business needs and how to measure the success of these. Furthermore, you will have a proper process in place to ensure that you are buying the right tools for the right reason and not making ad hoc purchases based on what others are doing. You are now following a plan with clear objectives that you can align to as a business but ensuring that you are reviewing this at regular intervals. Remember, you are not the one writing the strategy, there are specialists who can do this for you. You are understanding, challenging and finally approving.

Design

WHAT IS DESIGN?

From your Decide stage you should now have an approved 3-5-year strategy that you understand from a digital perspective and from a business perspective. It has been well communicated, and you have the buy-in from staff. It is now time to start executing that strategy in the form of the shorter-term plan in the Design stage. Here, we are designing the next 12 months of work in more detail than you would in the strategy. There is an old maxim of Proper Planning and Preparation Prevents P*ss Poor Performance, and this is never truer than of digital projects.

WHY DESIGN?

To hit maximum business value, you are going to have to work out an order of projects to deliver. This will be in conjunction with IT as there may be prerequisites that need to be completed first before you look at projects that span either staff or customers. You will repeat this stage a number of times as you progress through your programme of work. You should always be able to relate any project back to the strategy and the outcomes that you are trying to achieve. If you cannot relate the project to a strategy outcome, then you need to ask yourself why you are doing it.

You should also have a really good idea of the outcomes that you want to achieve with digital. Is increasing sales your number one aim? Therefore, we will start with making your Sales Team more efficient. Is it better customer service? In which case, we will start with that team. This is why understanding your business requirements during the Decide stage is so important as that will now help you to define the annual plan. Those businesses that jump straight into delivering projects without having done the necessary research are part of the 95% that are adding no business value.

Some projects will of course span an entire company. Maybe you want to deploy something like G Suite as your office productivity tool. That is a project that is going to touch every member of staff and you will only really see the benefits when all staff are using the system. It is a very different project plan to that of a tool that is maybe only used by Finance. Some of this will depend on how big your company is but you will always need to make a consideration between big and small projects and quick wins and slow burns. That's why Design is a key element of your plans.

DESIGN CASE STUDY

I rolled out Box.com to 2,000 people across an entire business. For those of you who have not come across Box, it's a digital tool that is used to store documents that allows you to share, comment, revise online and without the need to send emails with attachments connected. It can help ensure that you are all working on the same version of the right document. There are many other benefits, but throughout Discover you should have already found these. If not, you best get googling!

The ultimate win from Box was the removal of hundreds of emails with attachments, which at the time were all being stored on a server owned by the business. There was a no retention policy and, as such, the space and cost required to save these was growing exponentially each year. At the time there were 12,000 internal emails sent per day within the organisation. Imagine sending the same document to 50 people, those 50 people saving the document to their computer, but then also keeping the email with the document attached. We now have 101 copies of the same document being saved within the organisation's IT systems. Imagine you then revise this and, after having comments sent back to you, you may well have over 200 copies saved now. This was happening multiple times a day, every day. Box was brought in to alleviate this. The power of being able to share the same document via a link and, as such, only have one version, only really works when everyone is using the product. If only half adopt it then they can potentially only share with half the people they need to.

It was therefore essential that we designed a plan that broke the 2,000 staff down by units that generally shared with each other. It was necessary to have a senior management roll-out, as well as one that just went across the various teams. There were other teams that communicated a lot outside of their own teams too, such as HR and Finance. Working out what this needed to look like as a project plan was essential in ensuring the new system was adopted and we removed the plethora of emails travelling around the business. Those staff who work outside of IT often do not realise that this has to be managed and maintained.

The point here is that we had many small wins as we went department by department, which all added up to one big win over time. Not every project will be like this, but you can be both large and small in the same one. We ended up with a large corporate project that was broken down into much smaller wins with some teams adopting Box much quicker than others. The small wins, and communicating these, helped to deliver the big win. Designing a proper plan allowed us to deliver some elements quickly, some slowly, and generate more traction than we could without it.

STEPS FOR DESIGN

1. Design the plan

Using good project management software, you should be able to plan for the first-year projects based on pre-requisites and needs of the business. You will have a rough idea of costs, both internal and external. You will have a timeframe for the software implementation and then for the uptake of the systems by users. In a similar vein to the strategy, we are not expecting a leader to be writing the digital plan. You need to be able to see the level of commitment for time, money and effort and the outcomes to be delivered. It is this that is often misunderstood as this may have an impact on everyday work that needs to be completed. I have seen middle management halt projects part way through as they have not appreciated the level of investment that their team needed to make to ensure the successful delivery of the project. Nor the impact it had on their level of work.

This is why, as a leader, it is so important for you to understand this and make allowances for it. You may have to backfill a role in Finance whilst one of your accountants tests new systems and data. You may have a slower sales month as the new system comes on board. This should not be coming as a surprise to you. The focus here is on ensuring that you are reaching the end state from the strategy and ensuring that the ups and downs are accounted for, managed, and understood as early as possible. This does not mean that teams have an excuse to drop their performance levels, but there should be a tolerance level instigated. If the team drop below the tolerance level, then it may be time for you to step in and ensure that all parties have the necessary resources to get things back on track. If a project cannot be brought back on track, then you will also have decisions to make.

Sometimes, the delivery issue will not be with your business. It may well be with the company providing the tools and why it is so essential for you to focus your procurement on outcomes and, particularly, outcomes within timescales. It is another reason why you need to spend much more time on digital projects prior to buying any new tools. Sometimes it seems very straightforward, but often it is not, and this becomes a contributory factor as to why the industry sees such high failure rates.

2. Design with the users in mind

I once had to install a secure email system into a business. It meant that staff had to come out of their Microsoft email system and log in to the secure system that was encrypted. The recipient received a code to log in to the system and read the email. It was basic but worked well until the manager of a department came to see me in a rage. 'Your system has caused two data breaches in my department,' she shouted at me. 'Crap, how has it done that? It's meant to be fully secure,' I answered. 'Well, they find it too difficult to use, so they used their normal email and sent information to the wrong recipient!'

This brings us nicely on to the next element of Design, user adoption. Throughout Discuss and Discover you will have gained a valuable insight into the skill level of a lot of your employees and probably customers too. At this planning stage we need to consider how you are going to get staff to adopt new processes and tools as part of their role and how you are going to train them. Whatever time-frame you think you have in your mind for this, double it. It will always take longer than you think. I was once asked what the hardest part of delivering digital products was and I answered, 'the people'. I jokingly added that the sooner they built Skynet, from the Terminator films, the better. It is true, though – getting people to adopt new tools and new processes will take longer than you expect. It is much harder than setting the technology up.

The reason it's key to understanding this now is, if in the first year you know that you want to roll-out four proj-ects, then you should have a rough idea of not just how long the technical side of delivery will take, but also the people side. You need to know the resources and skills that you are going to need to help facilitate uptake. You will also need to think about communications and how you are going to get the message out to staff and/or customers and ensure that they have the right support in place. People are much harder to control than machines. Just ask Arnold Schwarzenegger.

3. Design your delivery method

In Decide we looked briefly at a small business case for your strategy that was based on the outcomes. This was to give you a rough price bracket to invest in digital tools based on the expected return. In this Design stage we will also need to consider one of the biggest choices that you will have as a business with regards to new digital tools.

There is a continual argument within digital around whether it is better to buy software or to build it yourself. Unfortunately, there is no right answer and it is something that you as a company will need to Decide. You will need to Discuss this with experts at the right time.

There are a few ways of looking at this. In simple terms, it just depends on the type of project that you are looking at. It is no different to choosing between buying your own ingredients and cooking or going to a restaurant for a meal. One will cost more, one might take a few attempts to get right, one may refund you if you were not satisfied, but you may be able to do it more quickly at home. It depends on your skill level and the skill level of those around you.

But, logically speaking, if you need to implement a CRM, then the market is flooded with these and there will be one that fits your requirements. You are not trying to enter the CRM market as a business so buy the one that works best for you. Most of the more modern ones give you a good degree of flexibility to configure them to suit your working practices. In general, if it is something for business productivity, then in most cases you should be able to buy software to meet your needs, or close to them.

Conversely, you may well be thinking along the lines of the airline industry and apps that allow customers to check in and download boarding cards. Here, you are more likely to be looking at the probability that you will need to develop a solution. Most of this should have become clear to you within the Discover stage as you may not have found solutions to some of the problems or issues that had been identified in the Discuss stage. If you are going to develop your own systems, then remember that you are looking at creating an ecosystem of digital tools. It will need to be built in a way that is complementary to other tools, software and plans that you have. If developing your own solution is the result, then remember to start with the data the app will be collecting and using.

Remember, though, that when you are discussing this option with IT or third party experts that if you ask someone who codes for a living what the best solution is the likelihood is that they will tell you to build something. Likewise, a salesperson will tell you to buy off the shelf. Again, go back to data efficiency and business benefit and that will help you to Decide which of the two routes to go down.

4. Design the project management

A consideration that you also need to factor in at this point is the actual project management software that you are going to use to run your projects. This is something that is often overlooked and left to manage via spreadsheets or focussing purely on a nice GANTT chart. This forgets that project data and the tools that you are using should be factored into the overall ecosystem of products that you are looking at. This may seem an odd concept to you, but as I keep reiterating throughout the book, we are primarily concerned with your business's efficiency. One of those concerns should therefore be project delivery efficiency. Not only are you going to be looking at GANTT charts to give you an idea of delivery timescales, but you should be able to look at all sorts of project data that will help you to learn and improve for the next project. Risks, tasks, prerequisites, spend, outcomes should all be monitored over the length of the project and reviewed at regular intervals and at the end of the project. Too many projects do not record project delivery data.

As I mentioned in Discover, data is the lifeblood of the systems that you use. You should be looking at how you use all data across your business. Do not forget project data. It is the only way that you will get more efficient with delivering projects. I have worked with a partner company VertoCloud for many years. They deliver exceptional project management software that also enables the business case to be included in the project plans so that measuring the success of the project at the end becomes quite straightforward. Whichever tools you choose, do not overlook this important element. Your

"

Do not focus on features that it must have; focus on the outcomes that it must deliver.

projects team also needs to become more efficient over time, becoming able to deliver digital outcomes more quickly and with fewer resources.

5. Design your resourcing

As part of Discover you should have been able to assess the level of digital skill that you have within your company. This will now be of benefit as you look towards your delivery plan. Consider whether these are projects that you will undertake with your current IT team or whether you will need to look for external support. The support can come in a variety of forms. It could be additional developers; it could be additional project management, change management resources, or you may want communication resources. Regardless of the resources you require, it is important that they are all familiar with the overall strategy and business outcomes before they come on board. This will ensure that they are the right resource and understand what the business needs to achieve. Obviously, any external resource will be an additional cost to your business and something to be factored into any business case. If you are bringing in additional resources, or even using third parties to deliver, then you will need to ensure that this is undertaken on an outcome-based basis.

I have seen too many projects hiring additional resources on day rates. This normally assumes that a project will take a certain amount of time but all too often it ends up taking a lot longer. Try to wrap any engagements up into the delivery of the final outcome so that you can ensure continuity and have a clearer idea of budget. This may mean that you as a business must agree to a certain level of commitment back to the resource. They cannot be held accountable for you not completing your tasks. You will need to ensure that you align things such as staff training and testing to meet the plan, making the right resources available at the right time. An outcome-based model will allow you to have more focus on ensuring delivery timescales. The same should be true of procurement of developers, development work or any software delivery. Do not focus on features that it must have; focus on the outcomes that it must deliver.

EXERCISE

The following exercises, advice, examples and space to answer them are all in your workbook. If you haven't got it, grab it at: **bethefive.club/workbook**

1. List 10 outcomes that you would like to achieve using digital tools.

2. With the list of 10 people you made in Discuss, assess their digital knowledge on a scale of 1-10.

3. Where are you on this list?

4. Where would you put most of your staff on this list?

5. If you have staff scoring under five, then list five things that you could do to help them adopt new ways of working and new digital tools.

6. Make a timescale for how you would like to implement new digital tools in your business to deliver outcomes.

7. How does this timescale compare to your digital knowledge scale?

These exercises are about finding the right pace for your business. All too often digital projects go at the speed of the technology being delivered and not by the end users. In other words, they are led by the speed of IT. Reverse this and find the pace that works for your business, based on your own users and how quickly they can adopt them.

SUMMARY

Design is a key stage that allows you to dissect your longer-term strategy into smaller, manageable chunks. It allows you to establish the right team, with the right tools to deliver really efficient projects. Not just efficiency projects, but project efficiency too. It allows you to ensure that the users are actively involved and engaged, so that you understand their skillset and the amount of time you need to allow for the uptake of the new systems and/or processes. It allows you to take a sensible approach to the different methodologies of delivery that will or won't work for your business. It allows you to ensure that you have a sensible order in which to undertake projects. Ensuring that you have the prerequisites in place to deliver the overall business aims before moving onto delivering those of the smaller departmental aims. You are now set to start delivering those outcomes.

Deliver

WHAT IS DELIVER?

Finally, we get onto the Delivery of the project. When you see all your work start to come to fruition. It's time for you to sit back and relax and watch as all the previous stages fall into line. It's the easiest of the stages for you as the leader... or, given that most projects fail at this point, it's the stage that needs just as much if not more effort than the previous four. Now we will be looking at moving away from that whole business level view that we have focused on in the previous four stages and start looking at each individual project in much more detail, ensuring you have the correct level of oversight. As a leader you need to be kept up to date with the project progress. You do not need the minute detail. You need to ensure that progress is communicated and that you are aware of the risks and issues as early as possible.

WHY DELIVER?

A lot has been written about Agile software delivery and Agile project delivery and the benefits of this over other methodologies. If you do not know what these are then please look up the Agile manifesto. In essence, though, what we are talking about is working in small incremental steps, usually about three weeks, constantly reviewing and iterating. The irony of Agile is that there are a whole host of people and businesses who stick to the methodology rigidly, which makes a bit of a mockery of calling something Agile. It has benefits, particularly over Waterfall delivery (again, look this up), but like all models they need to be flexible and to work for you.

The reason I do not give fixed elements to Discuss and Discover in this methodology is that it will change by industry, business size, age and goals. The methodology is designed to work for everyone and be adaptable enough for any type of business. How you then Deliver projects will again depend on your business, size, skillset, what outcomes you have purchased and timescales.

In Deliver we will look at how to allow your projects to Deliver by whichever model suits your business best, but still giving you the oversight that you require as a leader

"

Your IT delivery
team needs
to work at the
right pace for
the company.

to ensure the projects meet their outcomes. We will be looking at how to put together a project reporting template that works for your business.

Today, technology companies tend to deliver software through the Agile methodology. This is fine for the software companies. They can build software however they like. However, when it comes to your business you have to find what works for you. Agile often has large implications for the resources that you need to provide on a project. If you do not feel like you can cope with the resourcing or speed at which companies want to deliver, then do not. You do not need to follow the crowd. Your IT delivery team needs to work at the right pace for the company.

DELIVER CASE STUDY

I have worked with a local authority that had to pull the plug on a project after approximately nine months of delivery. It is not always an easy thing to do, and there may be other factors to consider, but in some instances, it is the right decision. It can upset a lot of people, particularly those that had worked on the project and new system for so long. If the service is starting to drop to an unacceptable level of performance, or the project is taking too long, then something must be done.

In this instance, the delivery company had continually missed deadlines, and this had put the authority on the back foot. It meant that the resources required to Deliver the project from the service were required more often and for longer than originally agreed. This had led to a lack of engagement around the resources at the middle management tier, which then led to decisions being made without the input of the service. The project itself was being led by the digital team as part of the overall strategy, who were pushing on without the department. The department itself was already struggling to manage its daily workload and, as such, could not afford to lose staff to the project as frequently as they were required. This meant that the project slowly collapsed on itself. Ultimately, the right decision was made to stop.

Therefore, fully understanding where your project is at is crucial to its success. The reports went to a certain level but did not go to the top. The information was not presented in a way that was easy to understand and to plan around and lacked the clarity required. The focus was purely on the timeline.

The strategy itself was not fully understood across all departments and by all staff, which meant that the benefits of the project were also then not understood. It had become a digital project led by IT. We have already looked at why this is the wrong way around. Here, though, they paid the price. Due to how the project was reported, the actual decision to stop was made later than it really should have been. If you cannot keep to a certain pace you need to be more flexible to ensure you can. There will be staff requirements and conflicts within their timetables. These need to be managed clearly and simply.

Setting realistic figures around time, effort, and cost when the original timelines were missed would have ensured that this project was either delivered effectively or shut down earlier. The authority ultimately wasted thousands of pounds in time and effort for a project that clearly was not going to be delivered.

In this section we will therefore give you a simple reporting template that immediately identifies issues, without relying on the more traditional Red, Amber, Green (RAG) status reporting.

STEPS FOR DELIVER

1. Deliver your projects

So how do you apply the Be The Five oversight to your projects?

In Agile the focus is on sprints. These are 2-3-week development cycles. I will not go into the detail of exactly what happens in each sprint as you do not need to know. This is one for your technical guys.

However, I dislike the term sprint, it is wrong and meaningless to those outside of technology and puts people off. In athletics a sprint is full-on, all effort, can go no quicker and be exhausted at the end race event. Think about a 100m race. We do not want that. Waterfall is more comparable to a marathon if you only saw the start and the finish. It is a slower but equally exhausting exercise. However, a development project is often just a number of sprints. We need to relate to something simple and easy to understand.

In athletics, there are many different types of race, and the first one, where it is a controlled sprint, is the 400m. Therefore, in this model we are going to work in races and laps. One lap of the track being 400m. We will relate a lap to being a week of time. Therefore, your project will be made up of a series of laps, that make up the race.

You do not need to keep the number of laps in a race consistent. You may Decide that the correct 'race' to run is for four laps (four weeks) initially to build the core of the product and then move to two-lap (two-week) races afterwards to gain better feedback on the key features. The choice is yours and depends upon what you are delivering, but you do not need to prescribe to a fixed time. Do what works for you. It may be a series of one-lap races, it might be five-lap races, or it may be a mix. Find what works and what you are comfortable with to be able to Deliver the outcomes you have looked at throughout Discuss and Discover.

For some technology builds, perhaps a rebuild of a website, you will not need to see anything for the first month at least as there is a core framework to put in place. Similarly, with smaller builds you may want to see developments weekly as you can achieve results quickly. This is one decision that is yours and does not need to follow a set rule book. Find a pace that works for your business. Not every company is a sprinter and not every project is a marathon. What is important, though, is that at the end of each designated race, however long, that you communicate progress to the business.

As the leader, if your team can report back to you based on the 5 Ds at the end of each race, then you will be in a good position to have a complete overview of the projects. Think of this as being the reporting layer above the developer or delivery layer. Give your project team the flexibility to find the right pace that works for your business.

2. Delivering the 5 Ds

Here is what you should expect to see in each element.

Discuss. Here your delivery teams can go further in depth and look at actual processes in more detail and how to improve these. This must be a joint effort with the users of the systems. Do not assume you know what the best process is unless you are involved in it or speaking to the right people. Do not underestimate the power of having proper, more detailed, conversations with people at this stage. One key discussion here is if any resources from outside the project will be required. This may be for testing or data checking. The resources and their availability should help you in Decide to plan how long this race is and potentially what in Discover is prioritised.

From a reporting perspective you will want to see who has been involved and what outcomes, processes and requirements have been Discussed. We need to see what resources are required in this race.

Discover. You have had the conversations. You have understood frustrations, pain points and poor processes. You know what they like and what they do not like. You can now start to pull this together into a list of requirements and outcomes. From the conversations you have had in Discuss, you should now be able to pull together a comprehensive list of these at a high level that will start to make sense from an outcome perspective. You can still iterate on specific functionality later, but the core outcomes you want to achieve should be well understood at this stage.

From a reporting perspective we want to see what outcomes the project is delivering and which of these are being delivered or part delivered during this race. Does this tie up with the resources available?

Decide. Any decisions that are made about this particular race should be collated here. The main decision that the project will make is going to be how many laps will be run in this race. Remember that one lap is a week of time. If you know that, based on Discuss and Discover, three laps are going to be required, then this needs to be reported. It helps the service managers plan their time and resources better if they know upfront who is required and when.

Reporting will cover any decisions that have now been made. How long is the race and how does this relate to the resources available? If there are any conflicts here, then you need to be aware of them. Do you have the necessary people available at the right time to Deliver the outcomes?

Design. This is where you are going to go into greater detail on how you are going to Deliver the outcomes of this race. No-one builds a house without designing it first, even if they change requirements further down the line. Similarly, there is always a sensible order to building a house. Start with the foundations and work your way to the top before adding the fixtures and fittings towards the end. This aligns nicely to having longer races early in the project and then much shorter races towards the end as the final touches that Deliver the best outcomes are agreed and delivered.

From a reporting perspective, you want to know and understand how they are going to Deliver the requirements and what you should expect to see at the end of the race.

Deliver. This then is the element of going away, doing what you have said you will do, and building or configuring what you have Decided and Designed in the first race. It is important not to dive into the Deliver phase of projects and it is something I see all too often. Going back to Proper Planning and Preparation Prevents P*ss Poor Performance, you need to ensure that you have an agreed plan that you can follow, even if it is just for the first race.

From a reporting perspective at the end of the race the report will be updated with what was delivered against what was agreed to be delivered. You will easily be able to see how on track you are or whether there has been any slippage. If there are issues arising with resourcing or similar, then this should be clear to you at this point. You can then take any necessary action.

Once your first race is finished, we return to Discuss.

In normal Agile terms, this would become a show and tell, where you are showing key users what has been built. However, the phrase 'show and tell' is one way. It must include a feedback loop and that is why it is not a show and tell as such, but another conversation. You could add another D here and go with Display and Discuss as that is nearer the exercise that you are going to be doing.

Once complete, you continue the Discuss phase into the next race period of the 5 Ds. It's a very cyclical method that ensures that you can bring users in at the right time, ensure communication is clear, see benefits as early as possible and gain an understanding of the people-change element of the project.

3. Deliver the race reports

What you will end up with is a series of reports that relate to each race within a project. To keep the language familiar to athletics we will call the project a meet. So, we have a meet (project) with a defined number of races taking part within it and each race is broken down into laps (weeks). You will have a high-level meet report that covers the overall length of the project and the overall outcomes broken down into smaller race reports. At the end of the meet you will have some comprehensive project information to use. Each report produced should be shared with your organisation. So, a 16-week meet could be made up of four races and each race is four laps. You would have five reports – one for the meet and one for each race. Alternatively, a 16-week meet could be made up of eight races and each race is two laps. Here you would have nine reports. The choice and flexibility is yours to manage.

Once the system is ready and you have built or configured what delivers the outcomes, then you are ready to deploy. Even at this stage, if the business case still stacks up to continue working on the build, then you loop around the Ds again and again until you have maximised the value of your delivery. You do not have to deploy software and then stop. The benefits of digital is the flexibility to constantly be looking at improvements and, as you grow to become more efficient, you will need to take advantage of this flexibility. Alternatively, you may not need to add functionality, but you may want to improve what you have already built. You might want to refine the system and make it even more efficient. You may want to stabilise the system and make it more robust. The projects do not always need to be about new functionality.

4. Deliver the benefits

We should also consider development costs of projects here. I have stated that you can continue to iterate and improve processes almost on an open-ended scale, if you so desire. This really must be looked at in relation to the benefits that it will Deliver. An important step to consider, particularly if it is a development project, is to know roughly how much you plan to spend on building your software. If you have a team of five developers and project managers and each costs you £40,000 per year, then with on costs of 25% that team will cost you £250,000 a year, or just under £5,000 a week (or lap in our terminology).

Knowing from the outset that you are going to spend £80,000 on build costs gives you 16 weeks to Deliver a system. The overall meet time is then the 16 weeks, which you will break down into races. The £80,000 number can be figured from the benefits that you will realise from the development. It might be about more sales, business growth, increased customer service levels or higher customer retention rates.

After 16 weeks you can keep going, but if every week of additional delivery costs you £5,000 in salaries and costs, then you need to be seeing the additional returns against this figure. One of the key terms that we need to be looking at as you get towards the end of a project is Evaluate. This ensures that you have delivered the outcomes for the costs and timelines and looks at whether further benefits could be delivered. Always take the time to evaluate your projects against the outcomes and desired outcomes. It is the only way you can measure success and know what the next steps should be. You will have your set of reports for the meet so evaluating against these is quite straightforward. Projects cannot be open ended, hence why you need to initially place a limit on this. You may Decide to extend the project to meet further benefits. The build might take longer than expected. You should have a figure as a starting point to work towards. Just be flexible where it makes sense to be flexible.

EXERCISE

*The following exercises, advice, examples and space to answer them are all in your workbook. If you haven't got it, grab it at: **bethefive.club/workbook***

1. Research Agile and Waterfall delivery methodology.

2. List 10 differences between them.

3. Why do most companies now prefer Agile? What advantage does this give?

4. Look at your current project reports. What level of detail do you receive? Is this enough for you to know that a project is delivering the required outcomes?

5. Is your business aware of the outcomes to be delivered?

6. How do you communicate this?

7. How have you measured success of a project previously? Is this celebrated?

These exercises will give you the knowledge of types of digital delivery methods and how you can overlay your own requirements on top of them. Focus on the business, the outcomes and success. If IT wants to build you a tool using Agile methodology then that is fine, but how you Deliver and deploy this to your business is yours to Decide. What do you need to do to make the project a success and what speed can you work at? The project updates you receive are vital to this.

SUMMARY

By using the 5 Ds as a project reporting template you can create a cyclical model of delivering your digital project that includes a sound decision making process. It allows for two-way communication at all steps and allows you to work at a speed that you are comfortable with. It does not prescribe what will work for you. As a leader your maintaining oversight of this is crucial; it is ultimately the stage that does or doesn't Deliver. You can apply a slightly different model to each project, depending on type and scale. By using the 5 Ds and working to laps in a race, then you will have a solid foundation for delivering the success in a way that the whole business can share in. You do not need to overcomplicate things. Keep it simple but keep informed.

BT5 Summary

You have now successfully navigated your way through the five steps that you need to take to understand how digital can help you become more efficient as a business. It is now time for you to stand up and be counted. Let us now dismiss all talk of transformation and place the focus firmly on efficiency. Your knowledge of digital should be somewhat improved if you have followed the five steps and completed the necessary work that you need to do to achieve success. You do not need to understand how it works, that can remain a mystery, but understanding how digital can help your business is crucial.

There is a lot to cover here but it is all relatively straightforward to achieve. You have five clear steps to follow that will set up your Digital Strategy and set you up to Deliver projects with real business value.

Go through the phases step by step. How much time you need to spend on each step will depend on a number of factors, such as the type of project, your current knowledge, or the size of your business. Really, you need to be spending enough time so that you are comfortable understanding each of the stages and how they relate to your business goals. You may need to spend less time on Discuss and more on Discover. You may be a smaller business and therefore Decide and Design may be shorter. There is no right or wrong. On the Be The Five foundation, I allow one month between each of the classroom days. This gives enough time to come to the next session with sufficient knowledge to make the day valuable and relevant to your business. This does not mean that it is the exact right time for you. You may need more or less time, and this will differ for each stage.

Do your research in the first two steps. Remember that you are not expected to write strategies or project plans. You need to be able to challenge and interrogate them. You need to be on top of your project delivery and you now have a simple template to follow. At a business level you have looked at:

○ Discuss

○ Discover

○ Decide

○ Design

○ Deliver

In Deliver you work through the 5 Ds again but at project level.

You also have a reporting template for your project team to report back to you:

○ Meet – total number of weeks to Deliver the project

○ Race – the number of laps being delivered as an increment

○ Lap – a week of time

Then have a report against the 5 Ds to keep you on top of the projects.

Meet	CRM Implementation – 16 Laps total
Race Number	3
Laps in Race	4
Races completed so far:	2
Laps completed so far:	5
Laps left to complete after this Race:	7
Discuss	
Discover	
Decide	
Design	
Deliver	

It really can be that simple.

What we are doing is building you a culture of communication. We are ensuring that the right conversations are had with the right people at the right time. We are ensuring that everyone is involved and understands the projects. Bringing the business and IT closer together.

Using this methodology gives you the framework to be in the 5% that adds real business value to your business with digital.

It is an ever-changing environment. We have got you here to understand the basics of your company and how digital can make you more efficient and effective. But technology changes constantly. New products are coming to the market every day. It is hard enough for people in the industry to keep up. It is why there are so many specialist niches.

To keep it simple, return to the strategy every 6-12 months. Ensure it is still right for the business. Return to Discuss and Discover to ensure that you are improving systems and processes. That you are helping your teams be more efficient. If you can always relate a digital project back to the strategy, and the strategy is founded on input from the business, then you will always be one step ahead of the pack. You will be able to pivot quickly. You will be able to see new opportunities. You can fundamentally change the way your business operates. You won't just be the one.

You will Be The Five.

Whether you have an in-house IT department, or you

use a third-party company, you must be comfortable speaking to them about technology. Talk to them about how it will help you achieve your business outcomes and be able to challenge them on their understanding of what your business needs. You have also learnt to put the focus onto the data that is the lifeblood of your systems and your business. If the tool does not do what you need it to do with your data, then it is the wrong tool. You have also learnt about product ecosystems and bringing systems together. A joined-up approach can not only help pass the data smoothly between systems, it will allow you to give a better experience to your customers, from prospect all the way through to valued and retained customers. You have learnt the importance of a good strategy that aligns to the business outcomes. It is some-thing that staff can get behind and the positivity that this can bring to the business culture through a shared goal is important. You must remain flexible enough to review and amend the strategy, as necessary.

You have then learnt about bringing that high-level long-term strategy down into a shorter one-year plan that you can monitor and measure progress against. Finally, we have looked at some of the different delivery models and some ideas that may help you internally. Remember that models are just that, they do not have to be stuck to rigidly. Find what works for you and stick with it. Do not follow a set of guidelines that do not work for you. Be adaptable and be efficient.

Although a popular phrase, culture does not eat

strategy for breakfast. The two are entwined and having a strong strategy will allow for that culture you want within your business to flourish. Culture with no strategy and strategy with no culture help no-one and are largely the part of strategies being designed in isolation. You have learnt throughout this book that working together with the rest of your business and with your customers will be what leads to not only a great strategy but also a great culture. Staff will be on board, seeing the direction you are going in and feeling part of the process. Not just a consultee at the end of a process.

Your staff and customers are your key allies in your business and working together with them will bring you the most value.

○ Discuss with colleagues and customers

○ Discover your options

○ Decide your strategy

○ Design your programme

○ Deliver your outcomes

Take your newfound knowledge and confidence in digital and use it to make your business the best it can be. Whatever your industry, you will become more and more of a technology company as you grow. Digital will play a vital role in all business.

PART

3

Becoming a confidant, impactful digital leader

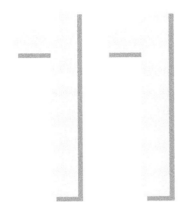

Your Digital Future

WHAT NOW?

So, you are now a digital whizz. You have got the world at your fingertips, so what now?

Now is the time to put this into practice and begin a lifetime of learning. Of thinking differently. Now that you have the basics you can start to think about the bigger picture. As well as providing digital tools to make your teams more efficient, or providing better customer services, you can now open up whole new avenues. You can utilise online services in the way so many did during the COVID era. You can change your business model. You can do more with video. More online learning, more online selling. You can change the way your company operates. If your most basic need is an internet connection, and that is ubiquitous and available 24/7, then location and time become irrelevant. Open your eyes to what digital can mean to your business and never stop learning. Think differently and challenge the norm.

You are not alone. You are a Synner. We work together. Constantly Discuss. Constantly Discover. Constantly Deliver. The opportunities are endless.

USING A DIGITAL MODEL

Leaders that are digitally savvy will ensure that their business takes advantage of the benefits that it can provide, but this is not just about the technology model. You can apply the same thinking to your business. Let me explain how thinking of your company as a digital ecosystem can help you to achieve this.

In 2016 I went to a conference in London for Box.com and one of the presentations was on Uber and the technology they use to drive their business. In particular, it was about the Uber app, which in its most rudimentary form is a platform to bring together a buyer and a seller. The slide showed how Uber had utilised several software providers, each credible in their own right, that when integrated together gave Uber the platform to deliver an excellent customer experience. It allowed them to grow and scale and be cited as a disruptor in their industry. The software detailed at the time was Twilio for communications, AWS for infrastructure, Google for maps, Braintree for payments and SendGrid for emails. All individual components were neatly integrated into this app and a good example of the whole being greater than the sum of its parts.

At Peterborough Council we replicated this approach with the same componentised platform approach with the digital tools we looked to move towards using. We broke down the various components of our IT infrastructure and had a common tool for each element, which importantly were designed to work together. We had Okta for security, G Suite for productivity, Salesforce for case management, Box for file storage and document management, AWS for infrastructure, Qlik for business intelligence, GoCardless for direct debits and a few other apps as well. Again, as per Uber, all these applications are fantastic as standalone apps, but bring them all together and they can perform much more effectively as a whole. They also had the added benefit of all being designed to work together, really giving you that ecosystem of apps that you could apply across the council.

It was all about breaking down the components and having a common answer to the problem that was reusable across departments and using the right mix to deliver individual services. It was the ecosystem of joined-up apps, though, that made the whole thing work.

What has this got to do with the CEO and your business model? What digital is bringing to the party is not just a new way of being able to deliver digital services but also a new way of organising your business. You will also have an ecosystem of teams, with each perfectly capable in their own right. But what if you brought them together? Would the whole be greater than the sum of the parts? Imagine if HR was Twilio, Finance was Braintree, Sales was Google, Marketing was SendGrid and so on. As individuals and teams, they all work perfectly well as standalone systems. But now imagine you could bring them together to create that Uber experience or team. Could that provide your customers with a better level of service? Could you align teams to products or services, rather than by job function, creating multidisciplinary teams all working together to provide the best service they can? They would all have an understanding of how each other operates and seamlessly integrate their work. Using digital tools, even as simple as Hangouts, Teams or Slack, can bring the right resources together to supercharge your service without making huge organisational changes. Digital gives you the opportunity to be flexible and to try new models without having to make big investments.

As a separate example, in football (or any team sport) you often hear the commentators talk about teams with less-skilled players playing as a team outperforming better teams with players that do not play in unity. We are talking about bringing forwards, midfielders, defenders and a goalkeeper together and integrating them as a unit rather than as standalone functions. The whole being better than the sum of the parts. Look at Leicester City winning the Premier League in the 2015/16 season. A team of largely journeyman footballers who came together to produce one of the greatest shocks in sporting history. A true example of the sum being greater than the parts and how pulling together as a team can bring big rewards.

So, whether as a football manager or as an organiser of digital components, as a leader you need to manage the ecosystem of teams and systems that you currently have, to provide the best experience for your customers. Using digital tools to bring your teams together with the right mixed skill set to deliver that Uber experience to all means that you can truly be the Chief of your Ecosystem.

As a leader it is important to reiterate that you do not need to fully understand digital technically. You do not need to go on a technical course to learn to code or understand how artificial intelligence works. What you do need to know is what digital is. How your business can use it and the opportunities it provides you. Being able to lead your business to digital efficiency will help you to meet your business goals. It is going to be one of the most important skills you can have as a business leader. I am yet to see a tender for management training facilitation that includes anything on digital. It is the one topic that is always missed. We teach managers finance, HR, and other skills but not digital. It is time to train yourself, all your managers and all your staff in digital, with a focus on how it can help your business.

YOU DO NOT NEED TO TRANSFORM

To reiterate one of my first points around digital transformation, this phrase covers a whole host of activity, but it mainly seems to refer to business-wide changes. In fact, the terminology changes constantly and now even covers how your business thinks or the culture of the company. It is all nonsense, though, and it is a phrase that needs consigning to history. The purists will shoot me down, they firmly believe in digital transformation and it being a way of life, but it is not.

Digital is about using digital tools (social media, internet-based services, and mobile devices) to enhance your business and to make real efficiencies. This may be internally about how you operate, or externally around how easy it is to serve your customers or for them to serve themselves. It is about using digital tools to grow rapidly, to serve customers better. For collecting data for better insights into your customers, and so placing your company in a position to be able to respond quickly to market demands.

As a leader you need to know how these tools can ensure the success of your business. You do not need to overcomplicate anything. Making simple changes and constant improvements will put you in the best possible position going forwards. It does not need to be difficult. You do not need to transform. You need to get better at what you do first.

Focus on the right areas of the business that will

make the biggest impact. Focus on efficiency. This can be across individual users, small teams, or the whole company. Stop thinking you have to digitally transform anything. Check those business plans, follow the methodology and align how digital is going to help you accelerate towards those goals. Remember that digital is not always the answer. Just uncovering poor processes and improving them is a step in the right direction. You do not have to do this alone. Being a Synner is all about working together. Use your resources and focus the business on communicating and moving forwards together as a whole.

DIGITAL CONFERENCES

I have spoken at a lot of conferences and I have attended even more. What strikes me most is the attendees' list and, more importantly, who does not go. You would expect as standard that members of the IT team will attend, that's a given. There are very few attendees from outside this sphere. How many IT or digital conferences have you attended? What is stopping you from going?

Of course, you do not need to go to every conference. I have left plenty very early as they do not provide me with any relevant information or are sold as something they are not and end up being trade shows. These conferences are firmly aimed at technical specialists and even I avoid most of them. The one conference that I have noticed that does have more of a mix is the Salesforce Dreamforce event. Here you have roughly 150,000 people descend on San Francisco for a week of learning and enjoyment. There is a good mix of technical events mixed with business-focused events. Anyone who runs a business would find value in attending this, not just around the software, but from all the customer stories and experiences. Salesforce are very good at putting their customers on the stage and sharing the work that they are doing and explaining why. Your knowledge of the art of the possible will go through the roof. Now, not everyone can afford to go to San Francisco for a week, but a lot of the event is streamed online. They follow Dreamforce with a World Tour and an event in lots of cities around the world. The London event is usually around the end of May and attracts somewhere in the region of 20,000 attendees. There is so much to learn in attending these events and seeing all the companies that provide complementary software to Salesforce and seeing a real ecosystem of products in effect.

Similarly, there are conferences in San Francisco for Box.com, and events in Las Vegas for Amazon Web Services with their Re:Invent conference and Okta with Oktane as well as many others. There are also many events across the world for these companies and AWS, in particular, has lots of events around using digital more effectively. If you plan your agenda well and go to the business style talks, as opposed to the technical ones, then again you will learn a lot and come away with new ideas that will help elevate you above your competition.

I have been lucky enough to go to Re:Invent a couple of times now and am amazed how much I learn about the services they offer. In my first year there I got to have a one to one, albeit with about twenty other people in the room, with Andy Jassey, the CEO of Amazon Web Services, and discussed the plans we had. It was an amazing experience to be able to share this with him and to pick his brain. It does show how these tools cross over a lot of the perceived boundaries between sectors. There is a tool for everything.

So please, when you are thinking about your year ahead and how you are going to be using digital, do not discount going to some of these events. You are not obligated to buy anything. It will give you an experience that you probably won't be able to get anywhere else and you will come back from the day (or week) with more learning than you have probably had in the previous two years. Do not leave it just to others to attend or to your IT team thinking that it will be techies talking technical. Absolutely some talks are, but there are a lot of talks on the agenda aimed at helping you improve your business and sharing the ideas of others. Use this to your advantage and learn from them. Be confident that you are right to be attending. Use these conferences as part of your Discovery. And just like the first time I spoke on stage and was terrified of being found out, they are there for you to learn. No-one is judging you. You may not understand all of it, but that does not matter. Listen, learn, Discuss, and Discover.

"

I want to work with
people who have
similar mindsets,
who want to achieve
something better.

INSPIRE OTHERS

Dan Price, the CEO of Gravity Payments, took a pay cut to enable all his staff to be paid $70,000 a year. This was the figure they established would give his employees the security they needed to not have to worry about money. They could then be more efficient and more bought into the company and its ethos. His employees ultimately rewarded him by buying him a Tesla from their own pockets to thank him for his sacrifice. That kind of leadership is ultimately what employees want. I'd highly recommend reading his book, once you've completed all your tasks in this one first!

When undertaking digital projects, are you the leader that adopts the new tools first? Are you leading by example? Are you making the sacrifices that your staff are having to make? Are you communicating with them? I am not saying take a pay cut but lead by example. Adopt new tools and new ways of working and embrace digital first. Do not force a culture on your business. Develop one naturally through leadership and thinking differently.

You have an opportunity to be an inspirational leader. One that adopts not just digital tools, but modern new ways of working. You have the ability to change the lifestyle of all of your employees.

But there is a bigger picture too. I have tried to align my business to two of the UN Sustainable Development Goals. The two I have chosen that mean the most to me are:

3 – Good Health and Well-Being

14 – Life Below Water

I believe that technology can help the world to become a better place, but it needs to be done correctly and for the right reasons. There are so many initiatives already benefiting from technology, from the charity sectors through to the environment. By coming together and focusing our efforts on some of the bigger issues we can really make a change. It needs people to become more digitally savvy, though. It's a self-perpetuating cycle of improvements that we can make. The more we learn and understand the more we learn and understand. I want to have an impact on the world. I want to look at the bigger picture. I want to work with people who have similar mindsets, who want to achieve something better. It starts with small steps towards learning new skills. New skills that will be forever useful.

FINAL THOUGHTS

○ Do not try and think / be like a digital start-up if you are not.

○ Do not get fixated on a backwards view of the working day.

○ Do not overlook your digital processes.

○ Do step up and lead the company through digital.

○ Do be a forward-thinking, innovative leader.

○ Do not worry that you are not from a technical/IT background.

○ Do not get left behind.

○ Do not lack confidence in making decisions on digital.

○ Do understand the outcomes of your digital projects.

○ Do make a difference.

○ Do work together.

○ Do be a Synner.

One Last Thing

One of the things I would expect anyone reading this book to realise is that you can apply the Be The Five methodology to absolutely any change that you want to make, whether business or personal. It is not just limited to digital or technology. Think about the steps we have gone through, Discuss, Discover, Decide, Design and Deliver. If you want to get fitter, lose weight, or you want to give up smoking. You can Discuss with others how they have achieved it. You can Discover what is out there to help you succeed, such as patches, gum, sprays, or hypnotherapy. You can Decide what your best course of action will be to help you succeed. You can Design a plan to help you quit: small steps, going cold turkey, cutting down a few a week. Then you can Deliver against this plan. As always, you may need to circle back to Discuss and revisit the steps.

There are very few changes that you may want to make that do not fit this model. I can take the example of building a house. Discuss what and where you want to build. Discover the type of houses and materials you can build with. Decide what you would like the final house to be. Design the plans with an architect. Deliver the house build.

We can go even further and look at a Formula One race. They Discuss the track, car, and conditions. They Discover the best set up during track practice sessions. They Decide on the overall race strategy. They Design plans and scenarios to race to. They then Deliver the race.

It's a simple method that can work anywhere for you.

For small changes you may want to link Discuss and Discover into one step, and Decide and Design into a second step, but you will always need to do all five. Although at the outset this book is designed for digital projects, take the methodology and use it to Deliver changes across all aspects of life. As they say in the Forces, Proper Planning and Preparation Prevents P'ss Poor Performance. Follow the steps, do the research, make the plan and only then can you Deliver against it, knowing you have got all the necessary information to hand.

Next Steps

You have made it to the end. You have covered so many topics that even getting this far is a real achievement. Not only have we covered the Be The Five methodology, you've completed exercises and research. You have looked at what digital can do for your business and why it so often fails. You have learnt that the most important element of this is communication. It is about talking. Learning. Listening. Knowledge sharing. And then having the skills and confidence to do something about it.

This is just the beginning, though. The strive for continual digital improvement will continue. It is not just a one-off exercise. After the first iteration of the combine harvester was produced to be pulled by horses we did not then stop. We have continued to modify and improve. We have added new technology and improved the efficiency of these machines. You will have to do the same. There is no end goal. It is a continuous process. The same with your learning. You do not just stop. There are always new things to learn and discover. New models to explore. New ways of making a real difference.

Join with me in becoming a Synner. Let's work together to improve things for everyone.

think **D**ifferent

be **E**fficient

work **T**ogether

be a **S**ynner!

Connect with Me

I f you have enjoyed reading this, then please do reach out to connect with me. I'm most prevalent on LinkedIn and it is the easiest place to reach me. My profile is:

https://www.linkedin.com/in/richard-godfrey-syncity/

All my posts have the #beasynner hashtag so please do follow it for all updates. Alternatively, you can look at either my company or personal websites. The addresses for these are:

www.syn-city.co.uk

www.richardjongodfrey.co.uk

The Syncity website has links to all my social media including my YouTube channel.

Details of all my speaking engagements, podcasts or other engagements will be posted on my personal site as well as LinkedIn. Alternatively, please do email me at:

richard@syn-city.co.uk

Syncity runs a series of foundations for business owners, CEOs, board members and senior managers to cover all aspects of digital technology. The three courses are:

BE THE FIVE

This six-month course takes you through the five steps of digital discussed throughout this book. Each step will be covered individually, providing the attendee time to complete coursework in between the attendance days and allowing you to build your knowledge through practical teaching and completing your own research. You'll be part of a community of Synners, supporting each other through the process, ensuring that you can come away from the course with a fresh insight into digital and the benefits it will bring to your company. This practical course will challenge your knowledge and immerse you in a new world of opportunity.

5D LITE

This course covers the same five steps as the Be The Five course but over two days. You'll cover Discuss and Discover on day one, with time between for your research before meeting again to cover Decide, Design and Deliver on the second day. This is an excellent course for managers and staff to attend to help them in understanding the full programme that you will go through as a CEO to ensure that you're delivering a strategy that helps and improves them.

GETTING DIGITAL RIGHT

This one-day course, primarily aimed at small businesses, will cover three steps of digital.

Prepare, Plan, Programme. It's an intense one-day course that delivers you practical advice in delivering technology to the smaller business who don't need to worry about scaling systems across multiple teams.

CONSULTANCY

Syncity also provide consultancy services in helping businesses in developing their digital strategies to ensure that you achieve efficiencies quickly and easily. With a no-nonsense approach to cutting through the industry jargon, you'll be well placed to move forwards efficiently and effectively. Syncity will work with you to identify key providers and tools that will help you grow and scale and ease the pressure of working with suppliers to deliver systems. Please see our website for details of our offer-ings.

Let's create a change in the world. Become a Synner. Help grow a Syncity.

Digital checklist

- ○ Ignore the jargon

- ○ Define the outcomes

- ○ Discuss and Discover are your two biggest allies

- ○ Models are there to be broken

- ○ Set your own pace, style and culture

- ○ Set your workforce free

- ○ Understand what you currently have

- ○ Know the skill level of your teams

- ○ Engage with IT

- ○ Know your business strategy, the digital strategy will follow

- ○ Efficiency, efficiency, efficiency

- ○ Lead by actions

- ○ Don't believe the hype

- ○ Find your own way

- ○ Ask for help when you need it

- ○ If you don't understand, say so

- ○ Never stop learning, technology changes fast

- ○ Be open

- ○ Help customers to help themselves

- ○ Automate the distractions

- ○ Think Different

- ○ Be Efficient

- ○ Work Together

Get a printable PDF version of this checklist at:
Syn-city.co.uk/book

Lightning Source UK Ltd.
Milton Keynes UK
UKHW012301290721
387926UK00003B/123